ACKNOWLEDGMENTS

Due to a variety of happenings, complications, conflicts and a general inability on my part to finish things in a timely manner, this work was long in the making. First and foremost my thanks go to my advisor at UF and the chairman of my supervisory committee, John Staudhammer, for his patience and his wry humor. Thanks go also to Eddie Sivazlian for his insightful comments, and to the other members of my committee -- Jack Smith, Joe Duffy, Jacob Hammer and Martin Uman -- for taking the time to review my work and suggest changes. Thanks to Greta Sbrocco, who handled the administrative details that came with my drawn-out progress, and to my parents, who impressed upon me the need to finish that in which I had already invested countless resources. Thanks go to Euphonix for providing an environment in which I could undertake and complete this work while continuing with my duties there, and to a variety of people at Euphonix who joined in discussions, tested new software, suggested alternatives, correlated observed events with our theories and provided relevant material. Among this group, special thanks go to Mike Morasky for the lively discussions we had concerning "the code" and his assistance in implementing many new features, and to Russ Kadota for his patience in interfacing his software with mine, for the use of his library and for his editorial suggestions. Finally, thanks go to my fiancée Christina, who is both the reason for this dissertation's delay and the reason for its completion.

TABLE OF CONTENTS

LIST OF FIGURES

LIST OF TABLES

Abstract of Dissertation Presented to the Graduate School
of the University of Florida in Partial Fulfillment of the
Requirements for the Degree of Doctor of Philosophy

SOFTWARE STRUCTURES FOR
DIGITAL REMOTELY CONTROLLED SYSTEMS

By

Andrew E. Kalman

December, 1994

Chairman: John Staudhammer
Major Department: Electrical Engineering

Digital Remotely Controlled System (DRCS) programming remains a potentially daunting task, particularly because of the scope of large systems and their requirements for reliability and performance. DRCS programming is not standardized, as the modularity of such systems often allows for a compartmentalization -- and hence an insulation from the outside world -- within which programmers can do whatever they choose. After examining how system architectures of the past have evolved with the arrival of inexpensive digital computing power, we propose an original, structured approach which yields benefits that are not immediately apparent.

We provide an overview of DRCS hardware and operation, and we illustrate how and why traditional, non-computer-based systems are often redesigned or replaced by ones which are software-driven. We introduce a new method for structuring DRCS software that employs only three basic elements -- state variables, I/O filters and commands. We examine a variety of alternate implementations within our scheme, and assess their effects on the system. Particular attention has been paid to the DRCS's observability from the outside world. We discuss how the often competing goals of reducing object code size and increasing execution speed affect the basic elements of our scheme. Solutions are proposed for the special cases where conflicts arise due to real-world issues that might otherwise compromise the regular structure of the software in our scheme. Finally, the methodology is applied to a large, complex system in assembly language, and an analysis is performed with respect to cost, reliability and benefits on both the methodology and on an implementation over its first several years of operation.

Programming a DRCS using our methodology requires minimum of 2-3 years of programming experience and a working knowledge of digital devices. This work provides the DRCS software designer with a new framework for creating a high-performance system that has tangible benefits over one that has been designed in a less systematic manner. Our focus is on larger systems, but the results are applicable to systems within a wide range of overall complexity.

CHAPTER 1
INTRODUCTION

Over the past forty years digital computers have undergone tremendous changes. The "world's first electronic general-purpose computer", ENIAC, developed during WWII, contained 18,000 vacuum tubes and filled a large room [Pat90, p. 23]. Today, the Motorola/IBM Power MPC601 RISC-based processor contains nearly three million transistors in an area less than two-tenths of a square inch [Tho93, Bur94]. In addition to the obvious improvements in speed, size, power consumption and cost, applications for computers have seen enormous growth. Computing chips, in the forms of microprocessors and microcontrollers, have become essential product design elements largely because they are an enabling technology with which the designer can provide useful features that were previously impossible or prohibitively expensive to implement.

Many new products are redesigned or repackaged versions of previous models. Adding a processing chip, the accompanying circuitry and sometimes a user interface (UI) can improve a product's functionality, reliability, safety, cost, size, appeal, interoperability, longevity, etc. Cordless telephones, digital watches, intelligent remote controls, test and measurement instruments, auto-focus cameras and automotive engine management systems are all examples of digital computing power serving as the enabling element to transform older products and technologies into competitive modern ones.

Internally, all of these products have an interface between the processing element(s) and the various parts of the product itself. Every such product has input and output (I/O) devices, some of which form the user interface, others which ultimately interface to the outside world. The use of a digital computer inside requires a digital interface between it and the I/O devices. This requirement has been accompanied by a great increase in the number and quality of analog-to-digital and digital-to-analog interfaces available to the product designer. The evolution of mass-market consumer items -- the compact-disc player being an excellent example, along with emerging digital-media recorders -- continues to deliver higher-performance, lower cost interface devices.

Many of today's products are digital-analog hybrids, and will not be replaced by purely digital ones anytime soon. On a human's scale of perception, the real world is analog, and a computer requires interface devices to interact with its analog surroundings. The scale of these devices range from large (industrial stepper motor) to small (airbag's piezo-electric g-force detector), but the nature of the digital interface to the processor remains common and recognizable.

With designs containing very large numbers of I/O devices, monolithic digital systems are easily overwhelmed by the requisite I/O traffic required to service the inputs and control the outputs. One solution is to provide a large number of independent computing devices which can, *in toto*, handle this traffic. While this approach can ensure adequate system performance, it lends insight neither into how the system's software should be structured, nor into how optimal a particular structure may be with respect to code size and execution speed. Coordinating the large numbers (often hundreds) of devices in such a system, regardless of the number of processors, is an unsolved problem. This dissertation provides a framework for designing and partitioning the software that operates such digital control systems. It focuses on the device interface and its impact on programming the host processor(s), and shows how this software structure is extensible to multi-processor systems.

A design based on the framework presented here has been completed to implement an expandable multi-processor control system for audio applications.

1.1 Digital Remotely Controlled Systems

In its simplest form, the digital remotely controlled system (DRCS) consists of a device with digital I/O, some sort of digital computer, and an interface between them. This device may take the form of a manipulator, a sensor, a switch, a display, etc. The computer will most likely be a microcontroller or microprocessor (μP), with memory. The interface will usually be a bus of predetermined characteristics. Together, these three components, along with a collection of other digital elements required to complete a working computer system, form a DRCS whose behavior is dictated by the capabilities of the processor, the properties of the device and the execution of the software. A DRCS will often be a new, application-specific design that builds on portions of older designs.

A DRCS can vary widely in scope and size, using a single processor running the simplest of programs, or with a multitude of processors running sophisticated operating systems. It can have one or many devices that interface to the real world. Interfacing to many devices with digital I/O, e.g. analog-to-digital converters (ADCs), is quite easily accomplished within the framework of today's typical μP system design. In the early stages of a design, the software engineer is usually concerned with issues like I/O bandwidth, interface correctness, and symbiosis between processor and design tools. Once the corresponding performance requirements have been set, a competent hardware engineer should have little trouble delivering a working prototype that the software designer can use to develop and test his programs.

1.2 Flexibility, But at a Price

As a DRCS's design, and later its implementation, progresses towards completion, some of the software programming decisions made will have a profound effect on the system. Earlier decisions concerning choices of hardware to match the requirements of the system will also have an impact. For example, some processor families (e.g. the Zilog Z80 series) can exhibit high performance when executing assembly-language code, but their performance may drop off rapidly when executing code compiled from higher-level languages (e.g. C). This may be due to a lack of availability of good compilers, or it may be due to the processor's architecture and instruction set. The freedom that arises from being able to design and program the DRCS must be carefully managed to guarantee performance.

Programmable components are often added to a design to improve flexibility and enable a wide range of operating modes. The benefits of this addition are quickly picked up by the system designer. In many instances, previously unrealizable features are easily implemented with the newly found power of the design's digital elements. The functionality and performance of a DRCS stem ultimately from its software.

Experienced systems designers recognize that the above mentioned power and flexibility are accompanied by a potentially negative aspect of the design; namely, that the success of the final product may hinge dramatically on the quality of the system software. Software that must interface to the real world can be very difficult to write properly, particularly when timing issues are involved, and a haphazard approach to a solution rarely results in success. Not only does the effort to manage software development increase with the size of the project and the number of programmers, but the myriad of processor architectures, programming languages, data structures and other programming issues make it difficult for many programmers to settle on a satisfactory coding paradigm.

1.3 The Software Engineer's Dilemma

Hardware designers can draw on a large body of knowledge outside of their own experience when confronted with a new design. Trade journals, applications guides, do-it-yourself projects, old schematics and data books all contain proven circuits which can be combined piecemeal to form larger systems. A thorough search can yield a near-limitless variety of solutions to a particular problem, many of which are easily comprehended and realized.

The software engineer faces a more difficult situation. Not only is systems software tied intricately to the hardware on which it runs, but the detail-oriented nature of control software resists simple one-page abstractions. While packaged software solutions are available (usually in the form of software libraries), most programmers find themselves utilizing some basic framework to which they attach task-specific software modules. Some such frameworks are newly designed for a specific project, others are purchased from software tools vendors and many are lifted from previous programming projects. The quality and success of a design have become largely dependent on how these tools are employed.

1.4 Good Tools Make a Difference

When searching for software tools, it is difficult to know *a priori* whether the chosen tool will remain adequate for the duration of the project. Only careful planning, covering all parts of the design, can ensure the adequacy of the tools chosen. Real-world constraints often limit the time available for this analysis. Furthermore, there may be unforeseen difficulties beyond the engineer's control, or the design requirements may change in mid-cycle.

> Even at this late date, many programming projects are still operated like machine shops so far as tools are concerned. Each master mechanic has his own personal set, collected over a lifetime and carefully locked and guarded -- the visible evidences of personal skills. [Bro75, p. 128]

Tools that provide the programmer with the ability to meet deadlines, achieve design requirements and work easily within the code are highly prized. Especially in larger, real-time DRCSs the ongoing coding effort can become overwhelming for many programmers. Common or standardized tools aid in communication, but specialized tools may still be required in certain instances. This work presents a powerful, general-purpose programming tool, in the form of a prescribed methodology, for structuring that part of a DRCS's software which handles the interaction between a processor and a remotely controlled device. Such a tool enables DRCS software designers to create higher-quality systems in less time, ultimately benefiting the success of their product.

1.5 Overview of Research

Thanks in part to Alan Turing [Tur50], the programmability of the digital computer means that a virtually endless variety of methods can be implemented to solve "any effectively solvable algorithmic problem" [Har87, p. 221]. Many approaches will be fundamentally similar, differing simply in the details of the implementation (e.g. choice of programming languages or size vs. speed optimizations). Our narrow focus on the digital remotely controlled device (DRCD), aided by the extent of standardized digital interfaces, will isolate us from needless details. The scope of this work does not include a cost-benefit analysis of every possible DRCS implementation, but focuses on the fundamental aspects of the interface between a DRCD and a digital computer, and how the choice of an underlying software structure to handle this interface can strongly affect the performance of the system.

We will analyze how the DRCD can be integrated into the DRCS, and its impact, direct and indirect, on the user interface. We will investigate the extent to which the specifications of the DRCD play a role in the design and performance of the system's software. We will propose a framework within which the programmer can structure the software of a DRCS to great advantage. Finally, we will demonstrate how this structured software approach can be applied to a large, real-time DRCS.

Software for a large-scale (hundreds of user inputs) multiprocessor DRCS that links the user interface indirectly to the DRCDs -- by means of processing elements operating within a particular software framework -- is the demonstration of the ideas presented in this dissertation. The goal of the research is to provide a universal and more formal framework for software linking user input to control output. A DRCS using this framework can achieve, at low cost, a level of small- and large-scale functionality beyond that of a direct input-to-output chain, and will allow for substantial expansion beyond its original scope.

Both new and experienced DRCS designers will benefit from this work for several reasons. First, it illustrates the benefits of transforming an older design into a DRCS. Second, it develops a well-defined structure for DRCS programming, a very useful tool. Third, it provides solutions for many of the real-world issues that must be addressed when situations force the designer to depart from his ideals. Fourth, it proves that a large and complex real-time system can use the proposed software structuring to its advantage. Overall, it enhances our knowledge of systems with digital control and builds a framework within which we can create robust, reliable and powerful digital remotely controlled systems.

1.6 Plan of Dissertation

> Particularly in assembly [language], you'll find that without proper up-front design and everything else that goes into a high-performance design, you'll waste considerable effort and time making an inherently slow program go as fast as possible -- which is still slow -- when you could easily have improved performance a great deal more with just a little thought. [Abr94, p. 3]

The impetus for this research was the observed fact that the development of a large, software-controlled system quickly becomes unmanageable if not planned carefully in advance; and success is unlikely unless said plan is adhered to [War90]. The sheer code size necessary to control and interface to a large number of DRCDs requires the programmer(s) to expend much time and effort to correct any repeated conceptual errors, to code desired optimizations and to enable new features. Without a structured approach to programming, we felt that progress in developing the DRCS would follow a line of diminishing returns. Hence we set out to characterize the basic requirements of the DRCS, and from them develop a framework for DRCS control software which would greatly ease further development and guarantee performance. By taking a "vertical" approach and accounting for all the DRCS activity that may surround a DRCD, we were able to create a design framework that is extensible "horizontally" to multi-DRCD DRCSs. The results obtained are widely applicable to all DRCSs.

This research evaluates the requirements of control software for DRCSs and the problems that the system designer encounters as higher levels of functionality are brought into the design. It investigates the interplay of software and hardware in such a system and seeks to define a software framework which yields the greatest benefits to the final product. It scrutinizes the software interface between the computing elements and the devices being controlled. It demonstrates the system advantages (and disadvantages) of divorcing the user interface from the DRCDs. It considers the ramifications of choosing particular software design constraints and methodologies. It analyzes overall system performance; furthermore, it examines those non-ideal situations where complications arise.

This research is organized as follows. First, the logical evolution of digital remotely controlled systems is outlined, and the characteristics of such systems are laid bare. Second, various schemes for organizing the software of such a system are evaluated, resulting in the proposal of a unique framework for DRCS software. Third, the framework is implemented within a commercial, salable product to demonstrate its utility. Finally the success of the implementation is evaluated, with suggestions for future designs.

This dissertation consists of six chapters. The introductory and background chapters survey DRCS fundamentals, expose the wide variety of DRCS implementations and raise the awareness of the great latitude granted the DRCS designer. These two beginning chapters stress the benefits of a well-structured approach. The third chapter presents an in-depth progression of a simple design from a traditional analog version to a fully digitally controlled one, and serves as a reference for the hardware elements of the DRCS architecture. The fourth chapter introduces the dissertation's central theme -- that of structured DRCS control software -- and details the steps involved. The fifth chapter covers a real-world implementation of the proposed software scheme, exposing the reader to issues of software-hardware integration, and concludes with an analysis of the costs, reliability, benefits and disadvantages of both the method of creating the DRCS software and of the resultant implementation. The final chapter summarizes the work and points out some directions for further development.

In identifying the objectives of this work, there may be some items unfamiliar to the user. These will be covered in depth later on. Our primary objective is to develop a framework, or methodology, for creating DRCS control software. Using this framework should lead to substantial simplification of the programming effort required. This framework should be clear enough for any first-time DRCS programmer to use as a guide for bringing his system into operation. A minimum of 2-3 years of programming experience, as well as a working knowledge of digital devices, is required. The DRCS programmer will be able to identify the defining characteristics of the DRCS and translate them into real data structures and procedures that fit into the proposed software structure. By the end of this work the reader will have an appreciation for the soundness of our approach, as well as the deficiencies of other methods.

We have two secondary objectives. One is to address the common worries of systems designers and demonstrate the tradeoffs involved in using our approach. We hope to convince the reader that our approach is simple, elegant, and enhances the performance of the system. Our other objective is to present and explore functional scenarios common to many DRCSs and show how the proposed approach facilitates bringing higher-level functionality to a design with an initial lower-level performance.

CHAPTER 2
BACKGROUND AND GOALS

The steadily increasing performance, falling cost and resultant proliferation of inexpensive computing elements, coupled with powerful, low-cost interconnect and networking schemes, has led to a digital control explosion in a wide variety of applications, such as automotive and telephony devices [Mil93, Cri93]. This was previously the near-exclusive domain of industrial controls; today, new applications are becoming increasingly commonplace.

The DRCS accepts user input and other external and system inputs and effects corresponding changes on (physical) target hardware in real time. Apart from monitoring the state of the system, the primary DRCS activity comes with user input changes; if the user makes no input changes then the DRCS may have little to do. When changes do occur, they can be fed back to the user in two primary forms: 1) an indication of the hardware change and 2) the resultant effect it has on the element being remotely controlled (e.g. robot arm position, audible signal level, engine performance). Only the creators and maintainers of the system are concerned with its internal structure. The internal workings of the DRCS must be hidden from the user. The system as a whole must feel as if the user is "connected" directly to the target hardware.

A very simple example of a DRCS is the emerging replacement with a digital encoder of an automobile's conventional accelerator linkage (usually a direct, mechanical linkage between accelerator pedal and throttle plate or "butterfly valve" on the engine). This encoder's signal is read by an on-board digital computer which then actuates servo-motor throttle controls in a predetermined programmed manner. These three items -- a sensor/interface, a processor and an actuator -- often are part of a much larger modern "engine management" system in which

- the user interface consists of the accelerator pedal, the tachometer, the steering wheel and various engine-status indicators (e.g. water temp and oil pressure dials, MPG indicator).
- external inputs consist of ambient air temperature sensor, fuel-air mixture sensor (so-called oxygen or lambda sensor), water and oil temperature sensor, manifold vacuum sensor, knock sensor, etc.
- a variety of analog and/or digital processes analyze the engine's performance and compute required corrections to achieve optimal power, economy, smoothness, etc.
- multiple digital remotely-controllable devices (DRCDs) like fuel injectors, intake plenum controls, ignition systems, valve timing controls, bypass valves, etc. effect the desired engine operating changes to achieve proper running.
- an external diagnostics interface provides a means of measuring and calibrating the system to a known reference.

Note that as a whole, we may consider some sophisticated automobiles as even larger instances of the DRCS. The new Audi A8 sedan "can sense where the sun is, and cool the hotter side of the car with more vigor" [Cor94, p. 24]. As an extreme example, one manufacturer has integrated additional features such as safety automatic windows, temperature-controlled seat heating, "automatic stability and traction control" (ASC+T®), "map-adjusted electronic engine power control" (EEPC®), "dynamic stability control" (DSC®) and "speed-related, pressure-controlled driver's side windshield wiper" into one complete networked automotive control system [Sch93, p. 26].[1]

In conjunction with the system's computing power the DRCDs in this modern engine management system provide the DRCS with tremendous flexibility and adaptability. The system in the above example can provide substantial increases in horsepower and fuel economy, a reduction in emissions and greater reliability and durability over engines without this level of control sophistication. The additional demands placed by a competitive marketplace often make a DRCS a necessity rather than a luxury or designer's plaything.

A generic DRCS system might be structured as shown in Figure 1.

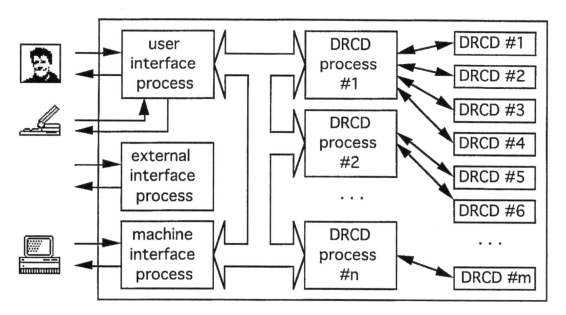

Figure 1: Generic Digital Remotely Controlled System

---

1 There is concern as to who will service such a complex automobile – its sophisticated electronics require training and familiarity beyond that of the average auto mechanic.

We characterize the DRCS as having the following components:

- a user interface (UI),
- a number of processing elements, performing a variety of tasks, and
- a number of DRCDs.

Additionally, the DRCS may also have, as an extension:

- a machine interface to enable connections to other computers, networks, etc., and
- an external interface to allow it to gather input from and disseminate output to its environment.

DRCSs have several advantages:

- They present the system architect and programmer with flexibility (for lack of discipline this can become a disadvantage, too).
- They are sufficiently modular to allow for transparent changes and upgrades to the remotely controlled devices (e.g. switching from 8-bit control to 12-bit control without altering the UI). This means that the software architecture of an DRCS can remain relatively independent of the hardware design.
- They are capable of instant resettability.
- They are capable of automation.
- The user interface need not be tied tightly to the DRCD itself. This has some Virtual Reality (VR) implications.
- Their cost is usually lower than that of less flexible architectures.

The hallmark of the DRCS is the insertion of one or more processing elements between the user and the item(s) being controlled. The existence of these elements and the resultant indirect link between the user and the target system bring a plethora of issues into a system that must appear quite simple to the user. The key challenge is to structure the system with an emphasis on the environment in which it will be used.

DRCS hardware is often application-specific, at least in terms of the interfaces and the DRCDs used. The choice of processing power is perhaps more standardized, but need not concern us provided it meets these general requirements:

- The processor(s) is a (are) digital computing element(s) with memory (e.g. Harvard or von Neumann architectures).
- In a multiprocessing scheme there is a high degree of interconnectivity among the processors.
- Software processes can exist transparently across one or more processors in the system.
- The interconnects have sufficiently high bandwidth.
- All the hardware in the system behaves in a deterministic manner.
- The hardware is sufficiently powerful and fast to operate in a real-time environment.
- The system is relatively easily extensible.
- As a bonus, the system should be fault-tolerant.

DRCS architecture and applications abound. Some are more suited than others to the task at hand. Given the existence of a hardware platform from which to build an DRCS, we will focus on developing structures for that software task which is unique to the DRCS -- the software that manages and translates user input to system actions and user feedback. We will analyze several DRCS scenarios and propose scenario-tailored software structures that are efficient, expandable/extensible and may have other potential benefits.

2.1 Review of Previous Work

There is a broad expanse of literature covering computer-based systems with heavy I/O demands. Among the topics often discussed are real-time response [Sta89, Oeh93, Tör92], architectures and partitioning [Mil93, Tan91], cost and reliability [Oeh93, Kir91], simulation and design [Fad92, Tör92] and performance evaluation [Mil93, Oeh93]. In most discussions of systems the issue of how to get from user input to device control is small. Of greater interest appears to be, for example, the investigation into why such systems fail [Inv93, Spa94]. I/O issues often appear relegated to the back burner -- the situation might be summarized by simply stating that "digital and analog IO modules are included for synchronization with an environment" [Kir91].

Given the little attention paid to the integration of I/O routines into these systems, we reasonably conclude that this portion of the design is generally being "hacked" without much attention to its effect on the systems. Suboptimizing by hacking[2] remains a viable means of achieving a goal; when used to excess, it rapidly becomes fatiguing to the programmer and detracts substantially from the readability, maintainability and portability of the system software.

> ... handcrafted assembly language and optimizing compilers matter, but less than you might think, in the grand scheme of things -- and they scarcely matter at all unless they're used in the context of a good design and a thorough understanding of both the task at hand and the PC. [Abr94, p. 3]

---

2 Using empirical data to optimize, as opposed to optimizing from an original structured plan.

Also, the performance of many applications and architectures is I/O bound [Abu86], perhaps without the knowledge of the designer. What is lacking from the literature is a systematic and formalized procedure for linking the input side of the system to the output side. The fact that all these systems use I/O, and that many of them employ a man-machine interface [Tör92], indicates widespread applicability for a formalized approach.

The lack of readily available treatises on this topic is perhaps explained by the degree to which it is hidden in the final product. For example, the 250+-page factory service manual for the Nikon F3 -- a professional computer-controlled 35mm SLR camera replete with DRCDs -- has not a single page devoted to any software issues [Nip80], despite the often-lengthy explanations to calibrate various subsystems to millisecond or millivolt accuracy. Neither do the brochures and user manuals. The details of DRCS software are somewhat akin to, say, engineering drawings for mechanical components -- they represent proprietary information that is not usually divulged. Without insight into them, the internal workings of a DRCS are neither glamorous nor obvious. Should they fail, it is unlikely that anyone but those intimately associated with them will be able to make any sense of them. Particularly in miniaturized products, the high repair costs make replacement a sensible option. Hence there is little incentive to publicize the DRCS software or to expound upon it.

2.2 Availability of Tools

What tools are available to create a DRCS? We must take into account that DRCSs come in many different forms, at many different prices. Examples are remote volume control, VCR cassette mechanism, numerically controlled machines, etc. Virtually every one of these systems is highly applications-specific, although some (i.e. in the case of VCR cassette mechanism(s), camera auto-focus system, etc.) have become standardized due to the immense volume in which they are sold. Most of these are small systems which have little or no direct user interface. They perform a rather indirect function, in that the user's exposure to the complex action(s) of the machine is masked within a simple action (e.g. focus the lens, eject the videotape, etc.). As such, there has been little impetus to extend the DRCS architecture beyond whatever is most expedient for the developer. The DRCS has in many applications become an "enabling element" of emerging new technologies.

This approach is acceptable if the product will remain static over its lifetime. Such is the case with Nippon Kogaku, Inc. (Nikon), whose camera models do not change over time, and whose offerings undergo leaps in functionality only when a new model is released. In this situation what is most important is that the product come to market quickly, function properly and be reliable. To this end, most well-managed companies have an in-house software programming methodology which seeks to reduce programming and software management effort and increase return on software investments by borrowing heavily from previous work. The familial resemblance of the user interfaces of several automotive, consumer and professional product families is an example of this practice.

Efforts are made to facilitate code migration from 8&16-bit (e.g. Z80, 68HC11) to 32-bit (e.g. 68000, 683XX, embedded PowerPC) applications [Mot82]. To a great extent the systems designers are familiar enough with newer hardware developments not to be discouraged when starting a new design. Designs tend to be evolutionary, rather than revolutionary. This is particularly true because experienced software developers prefer to recycle old, product-tested code than write new code.

With this pre-existing bias towards re-using parts of older designs, the software and hardware development tools[3] used to create DRCSs are necessarily a mixture of commercially available tools [McC88], in-house expertise and, on rare occasion, recent systematic advances. The focus of the commercially available tools does not currently include DRCS issues, as there is no established standard -- instead, these tools focus on well-known issues in software and hardware systems design.

2.3 A New Approach Must Be Sustainable

The shortcomings of such an approach are brought vividly to the forefront when user interface and interconnectivity/support issues arise. Within the audio market, for example, there have been numerous proposed standards [Que88], of which only a few have survived. Unfortunately, the quality of the standard has little to do with its expected lifetime, and market forces often play large and sometimes unexpected roles. Witness the Philips Digital Compact Cassette (DCC) vs. Sony MiniDisc (MD) fight -- many plants that were created for these much-heralded replacements for analog cassettes are now idle [Nor94]. As performance requirements increase, inefficient approaches are either abandoned, survive only at high cost, or are heavily revised to keep up within a niche market. It would be highly beneficial to have an approach that was resistant to

---

[3] One must distinguish software tools like compilers and debuggers, which help develop the product, from tools like kernels and libraries, which are an integral part of the system's software. The correctness and the performance of these "embedded tools" can be critical to the success of a system, and they must be chosen with care [Win93, Cat93].

or even obsolescence-proof against the inevitable changes that new technologies bring into the performance arena (resolution, speed, bandwidth, etc.).

Previously one might argue that, as computer-based systems and their attendant software are evolving so rapidly, any proposed software structure must rapidly become obsolete, or at least not be applicable to the next-generation product. We can now counter this by two factors -- the rise of platform-independent programming [Mey93, Neu91] and the gradual blurring of hardware-platform distinctions [Shi94]. There is optimism that both of these trends will protect intellectual effort and greatly preclude the re-writing of software for new platforms, as many software systems can now be ported from one processor family to another with minimal or no effort.[4] Thus the time taken to carefully structure DRCS software, and the experience gleaned from its performance over time, will not be lost when creating the next-generation version. Investing now in a framework for DRCS software will aid the programmer in porting to newer, faster and more powerful hardware.[5]

2.4 Chapter Summary

In order to be useful, a new approach to DRCS software must have tangible benefits. Also, the resulting design must be of high quality. As systems designers, we attempt to create "a good set of trade-offs from competing

---

[4] Of course, hardware differences (e.g. with plug-in cards) must be resolved when porting from one platform to another.

[5] Note that the actual coding of the DRCS framework will most likely be done in a portable language (e.g. C), and hence will always be reasonably portable [Hor90]. From a portability standpoint, the DRCS framework excels in helping the programmer support hardware on a new platform, as it insulates the vast majority of the code from hardware-specific compatibility issues.

objectives" [McC93, p. 165]. We will address that part of a DRCS's software which defines its functionality as the user sees it. This software will link the system's inputs to its outputs in a manner dictated by the system's functional specifications. In order to do this, the system must already have:

- a complete and error-free hardware design,[6]
- a basic software kernel that handles internal and external communications, interrupts, memory management, etc.,
- memory available for code and data, and
- functional specifications for the User Interface and all I/O activity.

In designing our DRCS software structure, our objectives are that the software exhibit the following external characteristics [McC93]:

- correctness
- usability
- efficiency
- reliability
- integrity
- adaptability
- accuracy
- robustness

Additionally, for the programmer's benefit, the software should exhibit these internal characteristics:

- maintainability
- flexibility
- portability

---

[6] Often this is verified through simple test code.

- reusability
- readability
- testability
- understandability

The method we present uses a well-defined structure to facilitate the creation of a DRCS

- which is structured and easy to understand;
- which can easily be extended, interfaced to, analyzed, monitored and/or built;
- which is accommodating to the inevitable changes and extensions that will be made to it over its lifetime in order to remain competitive;
- which is easy to maintain (from a software perspective);
- which isolates each part of the system from changes made elsewhere;
- whose hardware can be changed in number and type without fundamental changes to the underlying software structure; and
- with low replacement costs.

The DRCS software structure developed in the following chapters satisfies these criteria. Along the way, certain issues of software quality assurance and tradeoffs with respect to optimization must be addressed. We will show that this structure fulfills these objectives.

CHAPTER 3
DESIGNING TOWARDS DIGITAL CONTROL

Users who find a well-designed DRCS easy to operate may assume that it was easy to create. However, in the design phase, it is not at all immediately obvious to the programmer how the DRCS software should be structured to support DRCDs on both the input and output sides of the system.

In this chapter we present a simple electronic circuit, as it develops from one with a direct link between the user and the system's actions to the corresponding DRCS architecture with its attendant parts. This progression is best illustrated by example. We will see how the final DRCS reflects these developments.

3.1 Direct Analog Control

The example is one of simple audio volume control, in which the user moves a fader (a linear-throw, log-taper potentiometer) up and down to control the input signal level applied to a fixed-gain amplifier driving a loudspeaker. This example system is shown in Figure 2.

Here we have a user interface (the fader) which controls the volume of an audio signal. It is an inexpensive and simple system, but provides no means of obtaining any information about the system (e.g. total signal-chain gain or level setting) other than a visual indication of fader position (and hence signal gain) and an audible indication of output level. There is no form of remote controllability in this system. In this system the behavior of the system is dictated by the physical (here: electrical) characteristics of the devices employed.

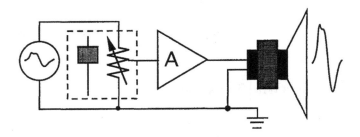

Figure 2: Example System #1 -- Simple Audio Volume Control

In this example some relevant characteristics are 1) the resistance values of the fader over its full range, 2) the gain, frequency response, noise, etc. of the amplifier, 3) the sensitivity of the loudspeaker and 4) the (power) supply voltages. Clearly, no software is needed for such a system.

3.2 Adding Indirection to Analog Control

The next step, as shown in Figure 3, is to add a level of indirection so that the volume pot is now controlling the gain of a voltage-controlled amplifier (VCA) instead of attenuating the signal itself. Conceptually this is the largest leap in the transition towards digital remote-controllability, for a remotely controlled device, the VCA, has been added.

This system functions identically to system #1, with the position of the fader giving an indication of the signal gain. Used alone, it has no real benefit over system #1. However, it allows the possibility of additional controlling elements (e.g. a separate volume trim) due to the fact that the amplifier's gain is now a function of the control voltage V_C. No information about the system is revealed beyond that of the first example. Note also that certain constraints are placed on the fader's taper (log) and on the VCA in order to map the user's positional input to the desired system signal gain. No software is needed for this system, either.

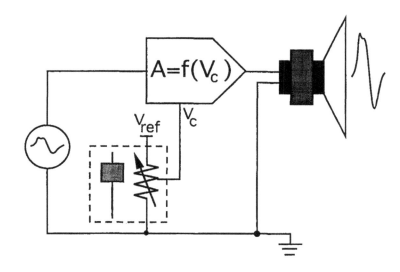

Figure 3: Example System #2 -- Audio Volume Control with VCA

3.3 Replacing Analog Control with Digital

By replacing the VCA with a digitally-controlled attenuator (DCA) and fixed-gain amplifier, we move into the domain of digital control of the analog signal. An interface from the user input to the DCA is required, and this is fulfilled by an analog-to-digital converter which samples the position of the fader and returns a corresponding digital word. Discrete control logic ties the two digital devices together. This is shown in Figure 4.

This interim stage in the progression from direct analog control to indirect digital control is of limited utility, primarily because the digital output format of the ADC must be a match for the required input format of the DCA. In order to be functionally identical to the previous example systems, together they must present a voltage-to-level conversion that is very tightly defined, and is thus rather inflexible. The designer will have to search for the appropriate hardware to complete this design, and may be unable to do so if he wishes to have certain characteristics (e.g. a "dead zone" at either end of the fader) that are not supported by the chosen parts.

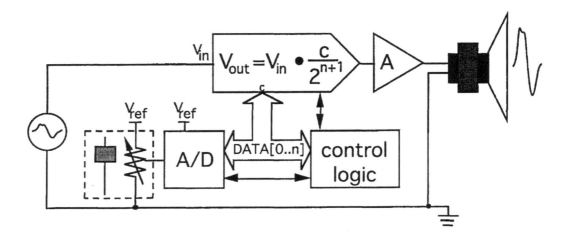

Figure 4: Example System #3 -- Audio Volume Control with DCA

We present this stage in the evolution of the system because the advent of the digital control word (between the ADC and the DCA above) signals the arrival of a level of abstraction, and hence a growing number of design choices, to the design. For example, the length (i.e. number of bits) of the DCA control word dictates the level-setting resolution of the design. We must also note that a choice of linear or logarithmic ADCs and DCAs for this example results in different data words corresponding to a particular level setting. As the number of interconnected digital devices grows, the number of possible implementations increases rapidly. This example system has digital devices without requiring any software.

3.4 Adding μP and Memory Provides Full Flexibility

Due to their low cost, it has become common practice to add a digital microprocessor (μP) or microcontroller to designs of increasing levels of sophistication. Using a μP to interface the various elements in Figure 4 enables the system programmer to link these elements flexibly, unlike a *hard-wired* design. What remains lacking in the above example is the notion of a storable *current state*, but this is solved by the addition of memory to the design. We cannot query the non-μP-based system as to its current configuration vis-á-vis the user input and the signal gain. Interfacing with the outside world is greatly facilitated by the μP's presence, as nearly all modern synchronous and asynchronous communications hardware are supplied with μP interfaces [Nat90].

Every μP executes a sequence of instructions, a dedicated software *program*. Creating software for DRCS-type systems is typically referred to as *embedded systems programming*. Generally a few years of programming experience is required to approach such systems, as familiarity with the system hardware (particularly I/O) and the more advanced issues of assembly language and real-time programming are required [Bec93]. A successful embedded system program incorporates a combination of many blocks of code; a kernel (perhaps with a proper operating system (O/S)), interrupt routines, memory managers, device drivers for I/O, etc. All of these concepts will be familiar to a programmer seeking to create a DRCS. Since these components are common to the vast majority of embedded systems, there are plenty of ready-to-use software packages [Buy94] and books to aid the programmer. What is not readily available is a structured method for tying the I/O devices to the rest of the system to create a functional system -- this is where the programmer's competency (and imagination) are tested.

With the addition of a processor, the hardware complexity attendant in a design can often be exchanged for dedicated software performing hardware-like functions. Programmability is added to a design to improve flexibility, lower cost, and provide for functions that were previously not possible. *Structured programming* [Led87] suggests that by following a set of rules governing the behavior of program activity (essentially forbidding *exit* and *goto* statements) program control flow is constrained in a manner that is beneficial both to the programmer and to the program. By adhering to a set of well-laid-out rules governing the interaction of a DRCS's µP with its I/O devices, the programmer has the missing tool -- a template of sorts -- to complete the system's software.

If costs dictate that we minimize the number of µP's in a more complex system (say ten faders and attendant signal paths instead of just one), it is likely that a single µP will have to service multiple user inputs. If, for example, two or more of these inputs are somehow linked together to control a single DRCD at the output, the µP quickly finds itself in the position of having to assimilate and make decisions on a large amount of user input data to properly control its DRCD (in this case, the DCA). This common situation can quickly exhaust the µP's on-board resources. In the following chapters we will show how this situation can be resolved through the use of a carefully-organized, memory-based software structure that makes extensive use of the current state or state variable.

This system's response must be sufficiently fast to prevent any noticeable delays between the movement of the fader and the change in signal gain. The sampled-input nature of the DRCS can of course lead to some aliasing problems, so we must typically structure the system to be fast enough for the application and to have ample dynamic range. This on-the-fly mode of operation is typical of DRCSs, and the structure of DRCS software can greatly impact the system's ability to continue running in real time when user inputs are changing at a seemingly high rate. The μP-based system is shown in Figure 5.

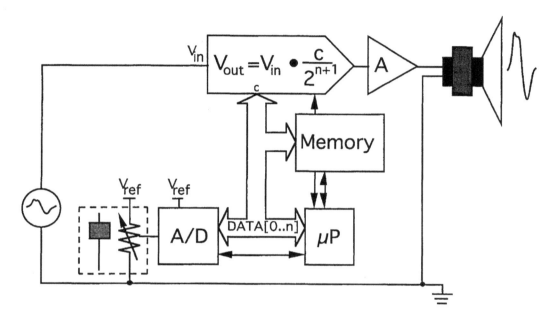

Figure 5: Example System #4 -- Digital Remotely Controlled
Audio Volume Control System

In Figure 5 we see that the addition of memory completes the example and enables the system to incorporate information pertaining to its current state.

Externally, this system functions identically to the first example, but we have now achieved some indirection through the flexibility to map any position of the user input to any desired gain (through a look-up table in the memory). We can choose a linear taper for the potentiometer because our concern is limited to mapping the position of the fader to the signal gain. This means that the μP's task is to read the user's input position and write the control word to the DCA in order to set the amplifier's signal gain. This also means that a variety of processing "tricks" can occur between the user input and the amplifier gain -- for example, the μP can apply hysteresis to the fader position coming out of the A/D converter so that the amplifier's gain does not "wiggle" unnecessarily due to noise in the fader. The key to this additional functionality is the addition of a programmable element, the μP, and its software. Note that we now have two entirely different representations at the A/D and D/A interfaces -- at the A/D we have a digital word indicating position (and, through table look-up, level), and at the D/A we have a digital word indicating gain as a function of the amplifier's make-up.

It is important to note that the nature of the DRCDs in a DRCS can be completely hidden from the user -- he or she is usually only concerned that the system functions correctly within its specifications. The details of the actual device (or devices) used to implement the DRCS's function are solely the concern of the system designer.

3.5 Chapter Summary

A powerful DRCS can be built up from systems similar to that in Figure 5. A DRCS will have a minimum of two DRCDs, and is likely to have differing numbers of DRCDs at its inputs and outputs. The number of processors used will depend on the number of DRCDs required, the task and the power of the processor(s) used. The software we are concerned with is the software that runs on these processors. There may also be additional processors not directly involved in the I/O chain, but they are not part of this discussion.

Sole reliance on the native format of the interfaces to the DRCDs employed limits design freedom. This is not to suggest that certain designs are impossible -- rather, a particular choice of hardware constrains the system's behavior to be dependent on physical characteristics of the chosen devices. For example, a particular D/A converter may have the desired LSB accuracy specifications, but the lack of a Gray-code scale [Hor89] interface may preclude its use in a particular design. Our goal is to create a collection of software constructs that allows the DRCS designer to integrate any devices he wishes to employ, and to do so efficiently.

Through this four-step example we have taken a simple, direct, stand-alone circuit and turned it into a digitally-controlled system with indirection and attendant complexity. We have shown why a designer would create a μP-based system with digital remotely controlled devices. As discussed above, apart from the flexibility obtained by divorcing the user input from the system output and inserting a digital process between them, there are a multitude of scenarios in which the system realizes substantial user-oriented benefits, such as:

- storage of current status, with ability to query,
- instant recall ability (snapshot),
- record and playback abilities (automation),
- remote (machine) controllability, and
- macros, etc.

In the following chapter we will show how to create the software that enables the system features listed above.

CHAPTER 4
THE DRCS SOFTWARE STRUCTURE

4.1 Division of Software in the DRCS

Figure 6 shows the DRCS with m inputs and p outputs illustrated from a software organization viewpoint.

The hardware layers contain devices that are unique to the particular DRCS.[1] The workings of the software layers form the basis of this dissertation. Every complex software-based system requires a directed and concerted programming effort to bring it to fruition. Whereas some parts of the system's software (e.g. an operating system) may be purchased or obtained in the public domain, others will have to be designed. A DRCS requires software interfaces to its DRCDs, as well as a body of software between its inputs and outputs. All of this software must be designed, and later tested and debugged -- the actual time spent coding is likely to be quite small [Bro75]. Unfortunately, good design takes time, may require much trial and error, and has no guarantee of success.

> Design is a sloppy process. It's sloppy because the right answer is often hard to distinguish from the wrong one. If you send three people away to design the same program, they might easily return with three vastly different designs, each of which is perfectly acceptable. It's sloppy because you take many false steps and go down many blind alleys -- you make a lot of design mistakes. Design is also sloppy because it's hard to

---

1 The flow of system input through the output DRCDs is required in those DRCSs that process non-digital data.

know when your design is 'good enough.' When are you done? [McC93, p. 161]

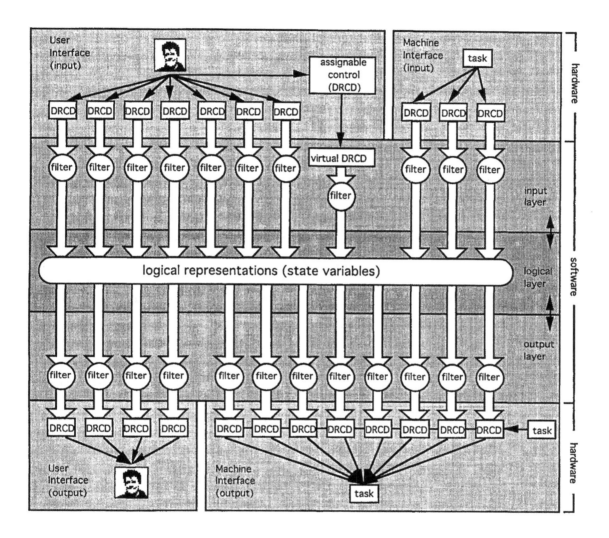

Figure 6: Layers within the DRCS

It is precisely this sloppiness that we wish to avoid. The lack of standardized design tools for such systems suggests that they do not lend themselves to straightforward solutions. We feel that this is not the case. The evolutionary design of our modular DRCS software structure has allowed us to implement and evaluate many different approaches to this problem. The initial structure was subsequently tailored through incremental changes to handle a wide range of operating conditions and requirements while still maintaining a high level of performance. The resulting DRCS has many internal features, the necessity of which is not obvious if taken in isolation. This DRCS structure should be viewed as a method towards creating a working system while minimizing software design and planning times. It will become apparent that there is considerable leeway within the structure to optimize portions of DRCS code for particular goals; "optimizing for size" refers to minimizing the size (number of bytes) of the system's object code, and "optimizing for speed" refers to creating code that requires the fewest clock cycles to complete.

Since the DRCS represents a melding of hardware and software, we must address issues concerning both parts of the system. We will first address the hardware issues that impact system software, for once the hardware is suitably well-integrated into the design, it can be all but forgotten and all attention can turn to the software.[2]

DRCDs are present at both the inputs and outputs of the DRCS, and respectively present and accept digital control data in a wide range of formats. The division of software in the DRCS is critical to the system, for by creating well-defined software interfaces for the DRCDs in the design, we isolate the tasks of collecting and disbursing control data from the task of processing that data. With this isolation each layer can be optimized independently.

---

2 In our experience, once the hardware interface was working, it rarely changed, and very few (if any) modifications were made to it over the course of the software's development.

4.2 Layers Within the Framework

As shown in Figure 6, we divide the system software in three -- the input, logical and output *layers*. It is helpful to view the input layer software as depositing into the logical layer information that represents the status of the system's inputs independent of the characteristics of the devices used. The output layer software can be thought of as extracting information to the output devices for the purposes of effecting system functions and providing feedback to the user. The software in the logical layer between them controls the flow of information from input to output. Note that since the inputs are sampled, there is never a direct path from the inputs to the outputs.

Associated with each layer is a *representation* of the state (or value) of its digital data. Some layers provide us with leeway in defining the representations; others do not. Prior to specifying the software of the I/O layers, in Table 1 we present the terminology involved.

Table 1: Layers and Representations

Layer	Representation	Constrained By	Design Freedom
input	input variables	input DRCDs	some
logical	state variables	standardized format	near-total
output	DRCD native	output DRCDs	none

The previous chapters' example has illustrated the general lack of flexibility with input format and DRCD native representations. This inflexibility arises from the design of the devices employed, and is inescapable. Rather than viewing this as a obstacle to the DRCS programmer, we will instead seek a means of defining the software in the input and output layers so as to avoid the limitations imposed by the DRCDs.[3]

4.3 DRCD Software Layers

4.3.1 The Input Layer

Input to a DRCS comes in varied forms. We need a clear view of the defining characteristics of the devices in the input layer before considering the structure for the logical layer. For example, consider the input devices listed in Table 2.

Table 2: Input DRCD Characteristics

Input Device Type	Interface Characteristics	User Perception	Choices for Interpretation
Knob or Fader	resolution, range	position, inferred function	incremental or absolute value
Key, Button or Switch	single- or multi-bit value	setting (perhaps context dependent)	ON, OFF or value
Key Matrix	multi-bit (format conversion likely)	e.g. as alphanumeric device	(none) or value

It is critical to understand how the input devices are perceived by the user (within the context of the particular system), and what sort of digital information the device presents to the rest of the system. Even when the user is presented with a variety of input devices, we need to minimize the number of different interpretations. A good example can be made with switchgear -- each switch, in

---

[3] We won't yet discuss the rare case when the input representation can map directly to the required physical representation.

- 38 -

its active position, should return the same value to the DRCS. Any deviations from this are likely to waste either code space or execution time. Sometimes this may require intervention in the early stages of the system's hardware design to ensure conformity. Of course, each input device must also be uniquely and unambiguously addressable within the DRCS.

Some examples of input devices and possible logical representations in a system using 16-bit data words are listed in Table 3.

Table 3: Input DRCD Examples

Device Type	DRCD Format	Logical Representation
ON/OFF switch	OFF: xxxxxxxx xxxxxxx0b ON: xxxxxxxx xxxxxxx1b	OFF: 0 ON: 1
16-position rotary switch	1st pos.: xxx0h 2nd pos.: xxx1h ... 16th pos.: xxxFh	1st pos.: 0000b 2nd pos.: 0001b ... 16th pos.: 1111b
vertical fader representing position, sampled via 12-bit ADC	top: xxxx0000 00000000b ... bottom: xxxx1111 11111111b	top: 0000 00000000b ... bottom: 1111 11111111b
potentiometer selecting one of three modes, sampled via n-bit ADC (n>2), 2^n discrete values	full ccw: uuuuh ... mid-range: vvvvh ... full cw: wwwwh	mode 1: 1 mode 2: 2 mode 3: 3

The first three examples are straightforward and safe -- they are the direct outputs of the DRCDs themselves,[4] presented one-for-one on a multi-bit data bus. The fourth example is quite different, in that it no longer bears a direct relation to the DRCD, but is rather a filtered version of the ADC's output. This

[4] Here we consider the DRCD to be the combination of the input device and the ADC.

filtering is performed in software, and produces a representation that is convenient for us when applying the desired action of the input device to the system. In pseudocode, the software filter for this example could look something like:

```
if (0 <= DRCD value < 2n/3) then return (1)
  else if (2n/3 <= DRCD value < 2n+1/3) then return (2)
    else return (3)
```

Some input devices will require only the simplest of filters, namely:

```
return (DRCD_value)
```

There are three steps necessary for the creation of the input layer software:

- create the representations that relate user action to system activity,
- identify the DRCDs and the values they present to the system, and
- create filters to translate the DRCD formats to logical representations.

By characterizing the data format of the system's input devices, and maintaining conformity among them, we can classify them into types and associate them with particular input-layer filters. This organization contributes to sound design practice, because too many DRCDs can introduce headaches quite apart from the issues we address here. Each input's ultimate representation (i.e. the output of its filter) should be expressed in terms that correspond to the user interface and the functionality of the system. Reducing the number of representations will naturally reduce the number of filters required. Virtual DRCDs are discussed in a following section.

4.3.2 The Output Layer

The variety of DRCD digital interfaces is vast. As with the input layer, we need a clear view of the defining characteristics of the devices in the output layer. However, we are no longer concerned with the devices' user perception and choices for interpretation, as the former is irrelevant with the device hidden from the user, and the latter is strictly defined by the device and the (sub-)system within which it resides. Consider the output devices shown in Table 4.

Table 4: Output DRCD Characteristics

Output Device (DRCD) Type	Interface Characteristics
DCA	word length, polarity, effect on circuit
Lamp Driver or LED	polarity
Relay	polarity, monostable or bistable
Pixel-Based Display	x- and y-bounds, pixel color requirements

As with the input layer, observe the same caveats when organizing the devices in the output layer. Minimize the different types of output devices used, and standardize their connections to the system. Once the output devices are identified, collect them into groups with identical interfaces. Note that this does not imply that identical devices will be only grouped together -- within the larger context of how the devices are applied in the DRCS, there may be several different groupings for a particular type. For example, identical momentary switches may be used in both an operator control panel and within foot switches -- in the control panel, they may toggle something on or off, but in the foot switch, they might keep a motor running only as long as the switch is depressed (i.e. a "deadman switch"). The raw specifications of a device are irrelevant; rather, the emphasis lies on how the DRCD is used within the DRCS.

Some examples of output devices and possible logical representations in a system using 16-bit data words are:

Table 5: Output DRCD Examples

DRCD Format	Logical Representation	Device Type
OFF: xxx0h ON: xxx1h	OFF: 0b ON: 1b	relay, latching or non-latching
0.32: xxFFh 0.40: xxC9h ... 9.00: xx09h 11.6: xx07h	0.32: 0d 0.40: 1d ... 9.00: 14d 11.6: 15d	Q (i.e. 1/bandwidth) control of 2- pole state- variable filter via DCA
'0': xxxxxxxx 11000000b '1': xxxxxxxx 11111001b ... '9': xxxxxxxx 10011000h	'0': 0 '1': 1 ... '9': 9	7-segment LED digit display

In comparison to the filters of the input layer, in the output layer we map easily understood logical values to values suited to DRCDs. For example, in the 7-segment LED driver example, the pseudocode filter might look like:

```
switch (logical value)
    case '0': output (7-segment display, C0h);
    case '1': output (7-segment display, F9h);
    case '2': output (7-segment display, A4h);
    case '3': output (7-segment display, B0h);
    case '4': output (7-segment display, 99h);
    case '5': output (7-segment display, 92h);
    case '6': output (7-segment display, 83h);
    case '7': output (7-segment display, F8h);
    case '8': output (7-segment display, 80h);
    case '9': output (7-segment display, 98h);
```

Once again, some output devices may require only the simplest filters. We will follow a top-down design methodology when coding for the DRCS. What holds true for hardware design is also true for software that interfaces to hardware:

> We must approach hardware design problems from the top, remaining aloof from hardware commitments as long as possible. We must thoroughly understand the problem and must let the problem requirements guide us to suitable hardware, rather than allow premature hardware selections to force us into unsuitable design decisions. [Win80, p. x]

Creating the output layer software requires these three top-down design steps:

- create the representations that relate user action to system activity,
- identify the DRCDs and the values they present to the system, and
- create filters to translate the logical representations to DRCD formats.

4.3.3 The Logical Layer

Creating the input and output layers using the recommendations above may be, in some instances, nearly all that is required. In cases where the representation chosen is such that a direct one-to-one mapping exists between input and output devices, all that is required of the logical layer is timely execution of the associated filters. In the above examples, the ON/OFF switch and the relay employ the same representation, and hence can be directly connected.

As systems grow in complexity and other factors (e.g. cost and density) come into play, this neat one-to-one mapping becomes the exception rather than the rule. This may occur, for example, when multiple inputs control a single output DRCD. In this case an interim layer of processing may be necessary, combining one or more input representations into one more suited to output devices. In another example, a single output control may affect both output control and output display hardware, and hence a means is required for grouping the execution of these related filters. These and other topics will be discussed shortly.

4.3.4 Summary

By creating software filters for the input and output layers we isolate ourselves from the details of the I/O devices used, yet in no way compromise our ability to control the DRCDs. Integration of the DRCDs (hardware) into the design is complete when the filters all exist and are known to be correct. The filters protect the rest of the DRCS from the needless complexity that arises from the wide variety of DRCD control data formats. Chosen representations, with their associated data, form the interface between the logical and I/O layers. The data in the representations fully describe the state of the system's input and output DRCDs. The format of the representation should be closely associated with the control function being performed. A filter is required for every different combination of DRCD format and representation. Steps can be taken during the hardware design stage to minimize the number of filters required. The logical layer passes control information from the input to the output, and may process it as well.

4.4 The Structure of the Logical Layer

With the DRCS's input and output layers narrowly defined to provide interfaces to the system's DRCDs, the rest of the system's functionality must, by definition, arise from the actions of the logical layer. Having established the need for and the utility of input- and output-layer filters, we must investigate more deeply the role of the logical layer in the design of the DRCS. Niklaus Wirth, in his seminal book [Wir76], enjoins the reader to envision programs as the combination of algorithms and data structures. The programs that act within the DRCS's logical layer are dependent on data structures employed, and the performance of the system can be deeply affected by the choice of representations in the logical layer. In this section we develop the software for the logical layer.

4.4.1 State Variables

As mentioned in the previous chapter, we define the *state variable* as simply a representation of the current state (or "value") of some element in the DRCS system. Without the notion of a storable current state in the DRCS (in whatever form), we are severely limited in terms of the functionality that we can impart to the design. Not only does the current state allow us to query and display the status of the system, but it also can be combined with previous and next states, which may prove to be useful. The choices that confront us as system architects are which elements and what format to use. We will review the options in the volume control example of the previous chapter.

We can think of the user input as a voltage, an absolute position, a relative position, a gain, an attenuation, etc. Choosing a voltage as our representative needlessly ties the format to a representation with which the user has little or no link. The other possibilities are more viable, but at this stage a qualitatively superior choice is unclear. In fact, we can choose from a wide range of different representations from the input layer for the μP's "view" of the volume control fader.

We must remember that output-layer DRCDs, on the other hand, offer no choices whatsoever -- the system must present the DRCD with specific control words that the DRCD understands. This "end-result" representation is usually inextricably tied to the design of the DRCD and is often in a form unsuited for quick human comprehension. In the previous DCA example, the system must supply the DCA with values between $2^{n+1}-1$ and 0, which in turn attenuate the signal by 0 dB to $-\infty$ dB, respectively. The word length of the representation is tied directly to the DRCD. Note that as this representation is the only one suitable for the DRCD, it must always be present in some form or another in the DRCS, even if only fleetingly. This leads us to the first possible logical-layer representation at our disposal -- the DRCD native format representation. Such a representation would require only the simplest of output-layer filters.

The DRCD native format is usually so far removed from anything a user would understand[5] that its usefulness is severely limited, except for one case to be discussed later. If we were to use the DRCD native format to supply, say, a system monitor reporting on the signal gains throughout the system, our software would have to translate the representation to something more readable before it was of any use to us. Also, such a representation requires *a priori*

---

5 See the volume control example in Chapter 3: "04C1h means cutting the level by -38.02 dB?!?"

knowledge of the nature of the DRCD itself! This is highly disadvantageous, complicates the system tremendously, and fails to isolate the rest of the system when an DRCD is changed or upgraded to one requiring a different control format. Also, each instance of combining user input from DRCDs with different representations requires code that is unique to this particular combination, precluding the use of standardized routines to handle more complicated input-to-output mappings.

We must therefore conclude that the DRCD native format representation is not a good choice for the central representation of the DRCS's current state. Since the workings of the DRCS must be transparent to the user, the system architect has considerable freedom in choosing a representation for use in the logical layer. It is, however, instructive to step back for a moment and take a look at what the DRCS is doing. Recall that the function of the DRCS is to translate user input into control output. In many DRCS systems, the user is the driving force behind all DRCS actions! Choosing a representation that the user understands has several advantages:

- Querying is simplified because the state variable is already formatted.
- The actual format (e.g. signed 16-bit in 1/10dB units) can be chosen to fit comfortably within the confines of the processing power used.
- All other inputs (internal and external) can be standardized to the same format, reducing or eliminating the need for extra translation.
- Since the DRCD's native format is unlikely to be user-understandable, some translating is already required.

A third option for the representation revolves around the physical nature of the user input (e.g. position of user control). This shares several of the disadvantages of the DRCD native format, but does have a marked advantage in one area, also to be discussed later.[6] Also note that choosing neither the user input format nor the DRCD format representation means that some part of the system may have to perform format conversion on the system's input and/or its output. While format conversion will invariably detract from system performance, parallel hardware or software format conversion can be employed in both serial and multi-processor machines to yield very substantial speedups [Abu86].

In summary, the best representation for the logical layer is neither one taken directly from the input layer, nor one taken directly from the output layer. Instead, a representation that is translatable to those of the input and output layers affords us flexibility and enhances the utility of the system by being as close to the user's perception as possible. Maintaining the entire set of DRCS representations in memory, over time, provides us with a means of monitoring the state of the system. An overview is presented in Table 6.

Choosing a state-variable representation for the logical layer completes the specifications for the input- and output-layer filters, and frees the designer to concentrate on the additional functionality provided by the logical layer through its state variables.

---

[6] See Chapter 5.

Table 6: Comparative Advantages of State Variable Representations

Representation	Advantages	Disadvantages
tied to input DRCDs or tied to output DRCDs	input and output filters are simple	often difficult to comprehend DRCS not insulated from hardware changes DRCS requires translators between representation and output or input DRCDs storage requirements dependent on device interfaces external queries require a priori knowledge of DRCD particulars format of input DRCDs unlikely to match those of output DRCDs
tied to system behavior	number of representations can be kept to a minimum easily comprehended without regard to physical constraints hardware changes require only new corresponding filter(s) complete freedom in choosing format no translations required when combining data	may require many different input and output filters

4.4.2 Filters and State Variables Define the DRCS

It is important to realize that state variables can represent a minimum of information with which to control the DRCD. In the example of Chapter 3 we can summarize the entire system by the simple statement "state variable *signal gain* = xx.yydB"

Given that the relationship between the input fader and the signal gain, as well as the relationship between the prescribed signal gain and the DCA control word, are implicit to the system, this statement fully describes this simple DRCS. As an example, in order to obtain the fader position we can map the signal gain to the fader position via a reverse table lookup, and a forward table lookup can be used to find the DCA control word.

In order to structure the system and avoid ambiguity it is important that the state variable's format be one that has function-like behavior, i.e. in this example

$$signal\ gain = s[\text{fader position}]$$
$$\text{DCA control word} = a[signal\ gain]$$

so,

$$\text{DCA control word} = a[\ signal\ gain = s[\text{fader position}]]$$

and

$$\text{fader position} = f^{-1}[signal\ gain]$$

The functions s[] and a[] above are of course the input- and output-layer filters, respectively. As long as the functions s[], a[] and f[] exist, the state variable will fully describe the system. The transitivity implied above is guaranteed to exist by virtue of the same logical representation being the output of the input filters and the input to the output filters.

The relationships above are clearest in those situations where a single input device is mapped directly onto a single output device. In cases where the mapping is not one-to-one, the functions above become functions of multiple variables, to be discussed later. Note that the state variable occupies the only place in this input-to-output chain where the system architect has some discretion as to the format used. This abstract quality of the state variable is very important. This further reinforces the importance of picking the right representation in the first place.

It should now be apparent that a DRCS system can be constructed in which the state variable is the only representation of the system's current state that need maintain a temporal existence. This is because the current values of both the input and output can be obtained solely and quickly, via the functions above, from the state variable.

We conclude that in a large DRCS, composed of many smaller elements, independent or interacting, a necessary and sufficient set of parameters that describe the entire system's state is composed simply of all the state variables, appropriately labeled. We refer to these parameters as the *current state*. Experience has shown that the memory requirements for state variables are often a tiny fraction of the total memory requirements for a larger system.

4.4.3 State Variables Enhance Code Modularity

The abstract quality of the state variable provides the systems architect with the opportunity to create modular code. If organized properly, the modularity of the functions that interact with the state variables and effect the input-to-output chain can be used efficiently in a variety of DRCS scenarios. In this section we will fully define how the input- and output-layer filters interact with the system's state variables. This interaction leads to the independence of the functions from one another.

For the input and output layers, for each DRCS I/O function, we propose a coding structure built around three simple functions: *set*[], *act*[] and *show*[], each of which is tied directly to its associated state variable. These three functions correspond to the input- and output-layer filter previously described. Set[] is the input-layer filter for all inputs, act[] is the output-layer filter for the machine interface, and show[] is the output-layer filter for the user interface.

The set[] function's sole purpose is to translate user (or other) input into state variable form. In effect, it projects new user input onto the DRCS's current state. For safety reasons, some bounds and/or validity checking should be performed at this point. The set[] function has no impact in the system beyond this action.[7] The set[] function may read and write the state variable.

The act[] function translates the state variable into a form suitable for the corresponding control output DRCD. It has no knowledge whatsoever of the status of user input -- it can only "see" the state variable, which defines all of its actions. The act[] function may only read the state variable.[8]

The show[] function is analogous to the act[] functions, but affects user interface output DRCDs. Through the show[] function we are able to indicate the status of the system to the user in a form that is easily comprehended. This is required in instances where the input user interface employs a DRCD that is

---

[7] Commands use set[] – see command section.

[8] Except in cases where a conflict between two or more state variables is detected -- in that case act[] may (over)write state variables – see Appendix A.

separate from the input device in order to provide visual or other feedback. The show[] function may only read the state variable.

In order to create a working DRCS, we require a mechanism in the logical layer to link the input and output filters. This we refer to as the *command action*, and it is the set[], act[], show[] sequence. A DRCS system may require one or many command actions to map user input to DRCD actions. Each command action is usually associated with a single state variable. A DRCS that solely links input activity to output controls need implement only command actions in its logical layer. The interaction of these three functions and the associated state variable is illustrated in the example below:

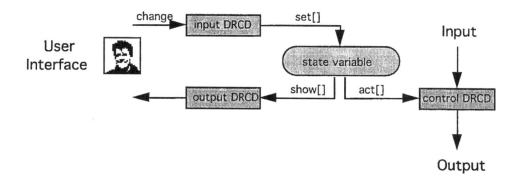

Figure 7: Command Action Flow

Note that these three functions are all independently callable. The thread followed when an input changes is therefore

```
set[state variable, new_value]
act[state variable]
show[state variable]
```

where the order of act[] and show[] could be interchanged if necessary.[9] The syntax for calling a command action is

```
command[arg1, ..., argn].
```

and is called the *command*. If all that is required of a command is the ability to redefine the entire state variable, then a single (perhaps multi-byte) argument will suffice. In those cases where additional control over the state variable is desirable (e.g. the ability to set or reset particular bits in a multi-bit state variable), a multi-argument syntax may be required. A command syntax can even be developed to accommodate a variable number of arguments. Whatever the command's syntax, there is one and only one command directly associated with each state variable.

A DRCS that is organized into multiple, similar sections or *channels* will require a more sophisticated scheme for allocating unique commands to its state variables. A hierarchical approach allows for many software components to be standardized, thus reducing code size and improving reliability. For a multi-channel system, the command format might look like:

```
channel_number
function_name
command_name
subcommand_name
arg1
...
argn
```

In a large system, hundreds of identical multi-bit controllers can be served by a single subcommand (as above) as long as the arguments specify which of the

---

[9] However, in this work we will always call act[] before show[], allowing us to make certain assumptions about program flow.

hundreds of state variables to act upon. Alternatively, the hierarchy of the command can make the specification of the state variable implicit through the execution of the command itself.

Each input-to-output chain, and hence each command, may or may not use both act[] and show[] functions, depending on the DRCS implementation. This command organization is itself no more useful than a single function to achieve the same end. However, other DRCS scenarios can make good use of this organization. We will investigate these next.

Table 7: Summary of Modular Routines

	set[]	act[]	show[]
corresponding filter	input (UI or other)	output (control)	output (UI)
state variable access	read and write	read only	read only
triggered by	change in input	change in state variable	change in state variable
special actions	bounds checking	conflict resolution	display of lock / unlock status

4.4.4 State Variables Form Snapshots

In a DRCS the collection of a complete set of state variables is called a *snapshot*. The system's current state is represented by the *current snapshot*. Snapshots are extremely useful. At the very least, they represent a compact, fully defined configuration for the DRCS from which all other input-output information can be obtained. We will explore some of their uses.

An important issue in DRCSs is *resettability*, the ability to re-configure the system to some specified state as quickly and as synchronously as possible. With this requirement follows the inevitable support of multiple snapshots within a system -- that is, the user can instantly choose between many different configurations with minimum effort. This is called *snapshot recall*.

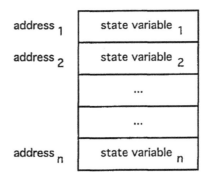

address $_1$	state variable $_1$
address $_2$	state variable $_2$
	...
	...
address $_n$	state variable $_n$

Figure 8: A Snapshot in Memory

When state variables are used and the input-to-output chain is organized on a set[], act[] and show[] basis, snapshot recall is greatly simplified. It amounts to the replacement of the current snapshot by a desired one (of same size and format, etc.), and then calls to all the act[]s and show[]s involved. We may or may not realize a speed-up over a system with single threads for all the input-to-output relationships, depending on whether the single-threaded system supported or was capable of the interim format of our state variables. What we do gain immediately is *synchronicity*, the option of controlling the DRCD update in a manner of our choosing. Once the new current state has been defined we can call all the act[]s in our system in any order, and then follow that with some or all of the show[]s.

Through the use of stand-alone output filters, snapshot recall can be structured for synchronicity by coding it as:

```
(re-)initialize all state variables
act[state variable₁]
act[state variable₂]
...
```

```
act[state variablen]
show[state variable1]
show[state variable2]
...
show[state variablen].
```

By grouping the act[]s (high priority) and show[]s (low priority) together, the delay between the invoking of the snapshot recall and the attendant changes in the control DRCDs is minimized. The action of snapshot recall can thus be biased towards the response of one group of DRCDs over another. This is altogether different from the sequential command actions required to achieve the same result:

```
set[state variable1, new_value]
act[state variable1]
show[state variable1]
set[state variable2, new_value]
act[state variable2]
show[state variable2]
...
set[state variablen, new_value]
act[state variablen]
show[state variablen]
```

The system follows this sequence of actions whether or not the command actions are split into filters or written as in-line code. Our scheme allows the grouping of DRCD updates, potentially preventing unwanted effects wherever multiple DRCDs work in concert. For example, an audio-control circuit may require near-simultaneous left- and right-channel DRCD updates, and undesirable artifacts may occur if the delay between the left- and right-channel updates is too great. This is a marked advantage over simple in-line coding of DRCS functions, and keeps code size small.

With the act[] and show[] routines the simplest way to initialize the DRCDs in the system is to perform a snapshot recall. It is interesting to note that snapshot recall can be optimized to call only those act[]s and show[]s whose state variables have changed since the last snapshot recall. This will require some sort of double-buffer state variable memory and tagging system.

When a snapshot is recalled, its state variables may no longer correspond to the current user inputs. We call inputs in this state *unlocked* inputs. The break with the user input that a snapshot recall introduces may require a means of displaying the correlation between the user inputs and the system's internal state. Unlocked inputs can be avoided altogether by separating the status indicators of the UI from the UI's input devices. In this scenario so-called virtual controls drive the system's set[] routines, and virtual display/indicators are driven by the system's show[] routines. A DRCS with snapshot recallability also requires a means of (re-)locking unlocked user inputs.

Some DRCS designers may be faced with the requirement of monitoring the correctness of their system(s) for safety reasons. Since the entire system configuration is derived from the state variables, the current snapshot can be sampled by an outside process for the purpose of detecting and correcting errors in the system. This supervisory potential of the DRCS might help to avoid catastrophic failures, notably in systems whose software was deemed error-free by its designers, but was innocuously used just outside its testing envelope [Inv93, Spa94].

4.4.5 Allocating State Variables

In a system with multiple DRCDs, where the mapping of input DRCDs to output DRCDs is not simple, we must address the question of how to allocate the system's state variables. Two issues arise: how to allocate those state variables that are associated with particular DRCDs, and how to fit the associated state variables within the memory provided. These issues are somewhat interrelated.

A DRCS may have one-to-one mappings or mappings of dissimilar order between the inputs and the outputs, as illustrated in Figure 9.

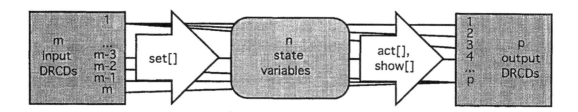

Figure 9: Input-to-output Mappings in the DRCS

As an aid to allocating state variables, it is helpful to describe the DRCS as a collection of the actions of its input-to-output *functions*. This is especially useful in multi-channel DRCSs, where many system functions are duplicated identically. Since our approach defines representations for state variables based on system behavior (i.e. input-to-output functions), we now address the issue of how to group related inputs, state variables and outputs together.

We will consider the case of a particular DRCS function, but it is equally applicable to the whole DRCS. For a given function, there are two different ways to allocate state variables; to tightly associate a single state variable with one and only one filter of each type, or to loosely associate each state variable with one or more filters, and hence DRCDs. The tight association is even applicable to more complex DRCS functions, as illustrated in Figure 10.

While this means of creating DRCS functions benefits from predictably simple filters, it is only applicable in situations where there is a direct 1-to-1 correspondence. It will increase memory requirements for state variable storage. Such an allocation scheme is contrary to our goal of defining state variables in a format which is independent of the DRCD characteristics. This scheme may also have detrimental affects on the design of the system, as it restricts flexibility in the hardware design stages. The inflexibility of this method of allocating state variables is apparent.

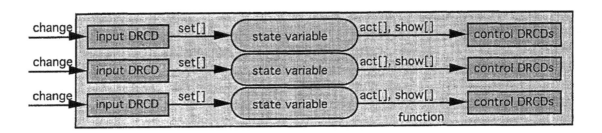

Figure 10: A Mapping of a Single DRCS Function Requiring
Multiple State Variables

The alternative is to use a single state variable for a particular function. Only one set of set[], act[] and show[] routines will be necessary, and each may interact with one or more DRCDs. Some examples of this scenario are illustrated in Figure 11.

These examples allocate state variables one-to-one with each DRCS function as defined by the user interface. In other words, each input-to-output chain has one and only one state variable assigned to it, and only one command. We are led to conclude that in order to allocate state variables properly it is necessary to associate them with the (high-level) functions of the DRCS, and not with the numbers or characteristics of the DRCDs themselves. It is the focus on the function, with its state variable and I/O filters, that is critical to the organization and performance of our DRCS software.

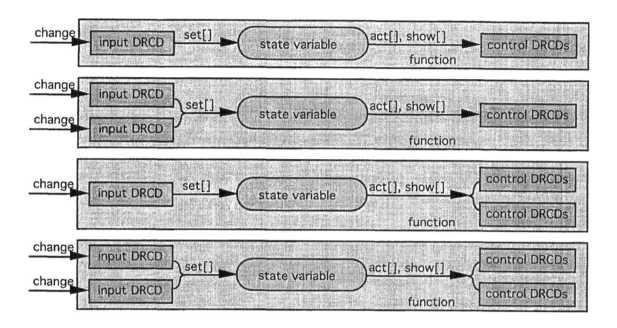

Figure 11: 1-to-1, 2-to-1, 1-to-2 and 2-to-2 Mappings of DRCD
Functions Using a Single State Variable

We must also address the different options for placing state variables in memory. Again we have two options; to pack them into memory as tightly as possible, or to freely allocate them in memory in a more convenient way. Arguments can be made for each scheme. In the former, as shown in Figure 12,

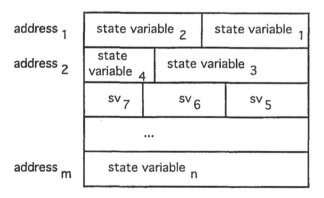

Figure 12: Tightly-packed State Variables

we can minimize memory requirements by fitting the state variables in their various representations into the minimum amount of memory. The disadvantage of such a scheme is one of speed and performance -- all parts of the system operating on state variables that share memory addresses with other ones must apply masks to read or write only the relevant information they are interested in. Bit-based operations could be used where the state variables are binary in value. Performance suffers even more if we try to squeeze multi-bit state variables into two or more distinct memory locations. This scheme also negates the advantages of the "one state variable, one command." Finally, the masking going on inside the system to support such compact state variables must be made explicit to any process outside the system wishing to use the state variables. These are serious disadvantages, and this scheme should be used only when memory is at a premium. A notable advantage, however, is that bandwidth requirements to and from the DRCS can be reduced with minimum-sized snapshots.

The alternative is to locate state variables in memory as one would put characters in a string, namely in fields of a contiguous memory block (see Figure 8). Naturally, this scheme does not minimize memory requirements for snapshots, though the wasted space is unlikely to be excessive.[10] Keeping the DRCS state variables separate from one another does have several advantages, which can be summarized by pointing out that any and all accesses of any type by any part of the system incur no additional overhead when reading from or writing to a single memory location. This is especially critical to those systems without built-in read-modify-write instructions, for in some systems the required

---

[10] The unused memory cannot exceed one addressable memory unit per state variable.

bandwidth to the state variables in memory can be very high during operations like snapshot recall.

It is also worth noting that the limited range of allowed values of the state variables may facilitate post-crash recovery by cleaning up solely the crash-damaged state variables [Tay86]. However, this is hampered by the fact that properly allocated state variables within a DRCS system are independent of one another and can change radically from one instant to the next (e.g. due to snapshot recall).

Table 8: Comparative Advantages of Snapshot Allocation

	Advantages	Disadvantages
strict 1-to-1 mappings	simple set[], act[] and show[] filters minimizes code memory requirements	very inflexible affects hardware design rarely applicable increases number of state variables
loose m-to-p mappings	universally applicable minimizes number of state variables easier to debug -- each function fully described by a single state variable	set[], act[] and show[] may need to support multiple DRCDs increases code size
tight allocation (minimum-size snapshots)	snapshot memory requirements are reduced system bandwidth requirements for external access are reduced	where state variables are combined in memory locations, masking and/or bit operations are required to access them external processes must be aware of used and unused fields within state variables
loose allocation (maximum-size snapshots)	state variable accesses are simpler simpler indexing of state variables to commands	increases size of snapshots

4.4.6 Reliability

The isolated scope of each state variables is chosen to wholly control one clearly delineable DRCS function. This has two major advantages: first, that if the validity of the state variable can be assured (outside the scope of this work, but crucial for any system to be reliable), and the filters are known to be correct, then the portion of the DRCS defined by this state variable is guaranteed to be correct. Second, the isolation of the entire input-to-output chain of a particular state variable means that the input-to-output chain can be created, tested and debugged independent of the rest of the system, and once verified as correct, need not be altered ever again. This localized activity of linking the state variable to the remotely controlled device gives rise to a central rule in the DRCS: that calls to act[] and show[] must accompany any change to the associated state variable.

Also it should be noted that among state variables sharing the same decided-upon state variable format, any error in code which employs the format should manifest itself the same way wherever act[] and show[] occur, thus increasing the odds of finding the problem. The worst problem areas *vis-a-vis* a breakdown in the input-to-output chain are invariably where an isolated, unique format was used and whose error was not discovered quickly due to the infrequent actions of that part of the DRCS.

4.4.7 Summary

The DRCS requires software in its logical layer. Because it is isolated from the input and output layers via filters, considerable leeway exists in creating this software. This isolation is enhanced by picking the appropriate representation for the state variables. Focusing on the user's perception and expectations of the system helps us develop clearly definable algorithms (I/O filters) and data structures (state variables) to achieve working programs (commands). We have found that structuring the software in this manner brings a number of benefits. The state variable is at the center of our approach, and its use simplifies filters, improves code modularity and enables us to form snapshots. Commands effect the desired changes to the state variables. There are a variety of tradeoffs to be considered when allocating state variables to the DRCS command structure.

4.5 Automation

A DRCS with filters to interface to its DRCDs, state variables to reflect the status of the system, and commands to link the inputs to the outputs is a complex system capable of powerful features such as snapshot recall and querying of the system's state. Of equal importance, however, was the requirement that the DRCS perform a more sophisticated function; namely, *automation*. The development of an automation system *per se* was not the goal of this work. Rather, in this section we will demonstrate how our software structure, built with commands, is highly suited to the demands of automation.

We define automation as a mode of operation in which the DRCS is recording new user actions and replaying previous user actions, synchronized to some pre-existing timebase. Automation must function in conjunction with the system's normal operation. As the timebase "ticks", the system tags user-driven activity with a *timestamp*. Then, by rewinding the timebase back to the start of the actions the DRCS can re-create the net result of the user actions so as to be indistinguishable from the original.

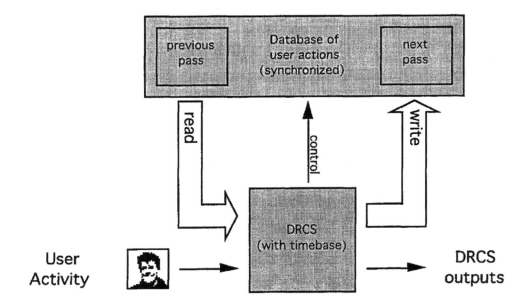

Figure 13: Automation (Single Pass)

Automation is especially well-suited to DRCS tasks that are completed incrementally, in *passes*. After each pass the last pass's automation database and the most recent user actions are combined to form the database for the next pass. The digital nature of the DRCS makes it particularly attractive to automation. Note that if the DRCS in question is one that accepts user input for action on something else, then that which is acted upon must also be synchronized to the system. The larger the DRCS's number of user inputs, the greater the potential usefulness of the automation system. On a large system automation is indispensable as it frees the user to concentrate on a particular part of the system while the other parts repeat previous actions automatically and repetitively.

From Figure 13 we see that at any time during automated operation the configuration of the console is a combination of what the operator is doing now and what was done previously. This is typical of layered automated operation. The DRCS itself need not be able to differentiate between current and previous operator input. The applicability of our command and state-variable scheme can be examined entirely in light of the link between the automation database and the DRCS. This is because the rest of the DRCS functions normally during automation. We must investigate whether the proposed scheme is well-suited to the automation database, and how the DRCS can readily accept automation data. Also, the existence of assignable controls in the UI may affect the design of the automation system. We will address the database question first.

4.5.1 The Automation Database

An automation system, and hence the details of its database, must be chosen to satisfy two criteria: it must fit within the current software framework, and it must meet certain objective requirements, e.g. speed and/or memory usage. Recalling that the goal of automation is to reproduce user actions, the most practical choices involve either recording user input (i.e. this button was pressed at this time) or recording changes to the state variables. Each has its own advantages and disadvantages. Recording DRCD values can be dismissed for reasons mentioned previously (also see Appendix B).

Having the automation database contain timestamped user actions, i.e. recording user actions as close to the source as possible, is desirable for several reasons. First, the accuracy of the system is maximized, as there is no possibility of a loss of information through the DRCS's input filters. We cannot hope to exactly reproduce user actions if we store state variables in the automation database, as there is not always a 1-to-1 correspondence between the two. The automation system does not attempt to recreate the operation of the DRCS; it seeks to recreate the actions of the user, and one might reasonably argue that its scope should be restricted to the user layer! During automation playback, the DRCS accepts user input both from the UI and from the database, so the input layer must be able to keep up with this ever-increasing load in order to maintain overall system performance. The information in the database is not sufficient to describe the state of the DRCS, only the activity of the UI.

A sample implementation of the database for this scheme is shown in Figure 14, with a record for each event containing a timestamp and information about the user input:

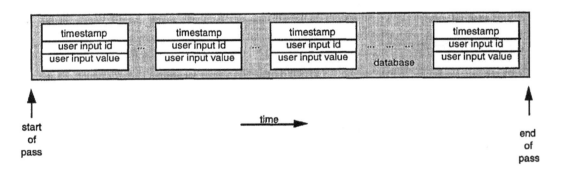

Figure 14: Sample Automation Database Format

The design of the automation database covers many issues that are outside the scope of this work, e.g. the timestamp information may be in absolute or relative time, and the database may be organized on a per-event or a per-timestamp basis. Here we are concerned with the information about the input events, and not how the database is organized or managed.

Recording user input changes requires a minimum of memory (since user input devices, particularly incremental ones, are often of very low resolution[11] -- switches are 1-bit, and positional indicators are rarely more accurate than 12-bit). Lastly, and perhaps most importantly, this method keeps the details of the DRCS completely out of the design of the automation system. Difficulties may arise when the automation system is expanded to include additional features that are related more to the function that the user is performing, rather than the way in which it is performed.

There is one area where a lack of DRCD-specific information in the automation system's scripts presents a problem -- namely, in the area of automated playback visualization. With exclusively user inputs in the automation database, there is insufficient information to see what the script's effect on the audio will be. We can, for instance, see the user's moving knob m from position p to position $p+\partial p$, but we cannot see the user's panning the signal source from left-of-center to right-of-center without a substantial amount of ancillary information (e.g. a map) about what knob m does (e.g. what it controls, what function it performs) and what its state variable represents. Oftentimes users of a playback visualization system will want this kind of information, particularly if the database is to be applied to another system of different design. Such information is portable if the emphasis is on the DRCS actions, and not the activity of the user himself.[12]

---

[11] Not to be confused with time resolution, which must be high enough to avoid perceptibility and aliasing problems.

[12] For example: "The edit decision list developed by CMX, Inc., is generally accepted as the standard in the video industry for performing automated edits. Other manufacturers (such as

In order to get around this, the ancillary information is usually contained within a map of the DRCS, which is either manually or automatically updated as part of a database in order to remain current with the DRCS configuration. Note that maps, unless structured very carefully with a strong bent towards standardization (e.g. w/MIDI [Mus85, DeF87]), become highly system-specific and non-portable.

Using an approach that records changes to the state variables has the advantage that the automation system can at any time fully describe the state of the system by creating a new current state from an initial value and the recorded changes. With state variables in the automation database the automation system can (re-)create the DRCS current state at any time without any action from the DRCS! This approach is better suited to those systems that are primarily concerned with what is being controlled, rather than with feeding back control information to the user. Since the database contains the history of each state variable, and hence each DRCS function, it is ideally suited as an aid to visualizing the behavior of the DRCS over time.

In order to make such a scheme work, a means of indexing state variables is required. As systems grow in size and complexity, the memory requirements for the index fields in the database may rapidly exceed those for the state variables. If memory considerations are important, it behooves the designer to develop an efficient format for the database files. The command format we have developed lends itself ideally to the needs of the automation database. The data fields in the database simply contain the command, which is really just an index, and the argument(s), which include the state variable.

Sony, Adams-Smith, Audio Kinetics, etc.) have developed CMX-compatible operating programs for use in their video and audio-for-video edit controllers." [Hub87, p. 286]

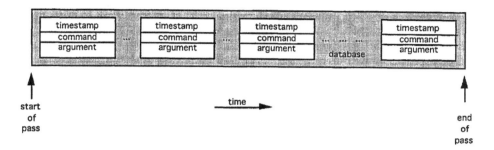

Figure 15: Another Sample Automation Database Format

The data contained in either type of automation database can be of relative or absolute form, each with its advantages and disadvantages. For example, the absolute approach is the considerably more fault-tolerant of the two, as the DRCS's state at any time t+∂t is not a function of its state at time t. Conversely, it is much harder to go backwards in time with the absolute approach, as all previous state information is lost when a particular item's state is re-written (absolutely). It should be noted that in some cases, where the recorded data does not represent some linear range of values, it may be difficult to create a meaningful incremental representation.

4.5.2 Assignable Controls

User activity through dedicated input DRCDs can easily be integrated into the automation system, using either the user input scheme or the state variable scheme. In systems with large numbers of identical output DRCDs, however, it is often advantageous and cost-effective to make use of *assignable* controls — controls that, through user actions, are assigned to a particular DRCS function

[Sta93]. Examples of assignable controls include function keys and continuous controllers (i.e. "endless" knobs). Such controls are typically re-assigned regularly to those DRCS functions that require the user's current attention. The context-sensitive nature of assignable controls destroys the simplicity of the user-input derived automation database, as the link between the assignable control and the DRCD must be stored as additional information. This also complicates visualizing the system activity through the database, as the context of the assignable control must be taken into account.

While a haphazard linking of assignable controls to the DRCS may be sufficient for non-automated operation, the demands placed on the automated system (efficient database, continued high performance, etc.) argue for integrating these controls into the system with a minimum of overhead. The solution to this problem is to create *virtual* controls (i.e. virtual DRCDs), one for each DRCS function that does not have its own dedicated DRCD. This is relatively simple, and requires an agent in the UI to be associated with each DRCS command. This way, the assignable control passes its new value(s) onto the virtual DRCD, which is then recorded in the automation database. Much of the coding for an assignable control involves mimicking the characteristics of the virtual control so as to appear correct to the user. The activity of the agent is what is finally recorded in the automation database. Assignable controls have no effect on the state-variable-based automation database.

4.5.3 Automating the DRCS

The above mentioned issues affect the automation database. We now turn to the underlying software structure of the DRCS, and we find that the command structure is well suited to handle the demands of automation, assignable controls and concurrent user activity. This is because it ultimately provides a single, simple entry point (the command) for the recorded event to enter the system and reproduce the original action, this time without user input.

A significant performance increase can be obtained in situations where the system's DRCDs need only be updated at a prescribed time, as opposed to continuously. This is done by performing only the set[] portion of commands until the DRCDs need updating, whereupon the act[] and show[] portions of a snapshot recall are performed. This is possible because the state variable, which the set[] portion of the commands is modifying, is the only item required to fully define the state of the system. Of course, performing set[] without act[] leaves us with a system whose DRCDs do not correctly correspond to their state variables, i.e. they are unlocked. In some situations this may be acceptable as a tradeoff towards better performance as long as the DRCDs are ultimately locked.

4.5.4 Summary

Within the proposed DRCS automation can be implemented in two distinct ways, each with its advantages. The DRCS can accommodate either scheme, for the user-input-based scheme can be wholly isolated from the workings of the DRCS, and the state-variable-based scheme is intimately associated with the system's current state. Both can be implemented with commands. DRCS functions without dedicated DRCDs in the user interface require virtual DRCDs. The larger the DRCS, the greater the need for a command organization. The approaches to automation are summarized below:

Table 9: Comparative Advantages of DRCS Automation Schemes

	User-Input Based	State-Variable Based
accuracy in replaying user actions	perfect	may lose resolution where no 1-to-1 mapping exists between user input and state variable
load on DRCS	DRCS must interpret automation data as additional user actions, using some of its power; stays constant	automation data bypasses user input and is executed solely as commands; less predictable
possible data formats	incremental and absolute	incremental and absolute
automation database	provides information on state of user input transportable to other systems only through a map for translation	provides information on DRCS state potentially transportable to other systems
feedback on input devices of previous passes	easier to implement	more difficult to implement

4.6 Command-Based Structure

Another advantage of the command structure has only become apparent with the enlargement of the DRCS's scope in software and operations. Those functions which require considerable inter-channel communications (e.g. a grouping of controls) can be quickly implemented once a standardized command scheme is in place. In any large system, it is possible to implement inter-channel meta functions in a variety of ways -- for example, channels could "talk" to one another (loosely coupled), or channels could communicate via a central shared piece of memory (tightly coupled). Often there are good reasons for picking one scheme over the other, and a DRCS may uses both schemes to its advantage. Some functions are much more easily realized when message transmittal and receipt are deterministic. Having chosen a state variable scheme which is compatible across different channels, as well as different types of channels, ensures that computational power is not wasted in data type translations and other types of conversions.

4.6.1 Executing Commands

Assignable controls and automation require a mechanism whereby the control activity leads to changes in the corresponding state variable. By adding a mechanism for executing commands from an external source, the DRCS is able to simultaneously accept and act upon user, automation and external inputs. As the DRCS workload increases, any command-execution overhead manifests itself as a deterioration in the system's real-time performance.

This part of the DRCS design does not lend itself well to a generalized approach. Rather, the DRCS programmer must consider the relative importance of many issues revolving around command execution before settling on a command format. For instance, dedicating additional bits to a command format so as to make destination addressing and sender notification easier will place a processing burden on all parts of the system that do not make use of this additional information. On the other hand, a lack of such information may preclude certain system functions that "handshake" between channels. With unlimited code space all actions could be performed as commands -- however, this way may be impractical or simply unnecessary (or even dangerous), as although a large number of actions lend themselves to being made commands, some actions do not. In any event, these issues do not detract from the applicability of our state-variable-based approach to defining DRCS functions.

4.7 Macros

Another notable benefit of the unified command structure is the use of *macros* -- small assemblages of data that provide the ability to replay a sequence or group of user actions with or without a time reference, respectively. Macros are especially useful for repetitive or complicated user actions. The DRCS must provide a means of creating macros, ranging from the conceptually simple but tedious editing of a text or data file to the complex (software-wise) but easy-to-use automatic recording of user actions. A DRCS built around a command structure has no difficulty executing macros or assembling user actions into macros. The macro can be viewed as the ultimate incarnation of the command, as it can exist in and be triggered and executed by any part of the system.

Macros have proven to be especially useful when the development of DRCS functions outpaces the development of the UI. With a macro, a function can be tested via its associated command and the chosen argument, without any UI interaction. While each part of the UI must have a command associated with it, the converse is not true. Test commands, for example, may intentionally be left out of the UI for safety or security reasons. Macros are an ideal means of executing these types of commands in the system. Grouped macros appear as consecutive commands. Timed macros can be stored in the same format as automation data as long as the timestamps are compatible.

4.8 Chapter Summary

A scheme for structuring software in digital remotely controlled systems has been proposed. By describing the operation of the DRCS in terms of the functions it presents to the user, an organization with distinct layers is achieved. Each layer contains distinct software, yet they are all tied together by the DRCS's central software entity, the command. Each DRCS function, from user input to control output, is fully described by its associated command. Commands operate on centrally located state variables, which at all times fully describe the state of the system. The system's ability to execute commands, as well as the independent nature of the components of the commands, can be exploited to create higher-level DRCS functionality with little overhead. With the command structure in place, adding new features and functions to the DRCS becomes simply an exercise in defining the state variable(s), creating the input and output filters, and assembling them into a command -- a relatively easy task.

Below are illustrated the three main phases of DRCS software design when following the method described in this chapter.

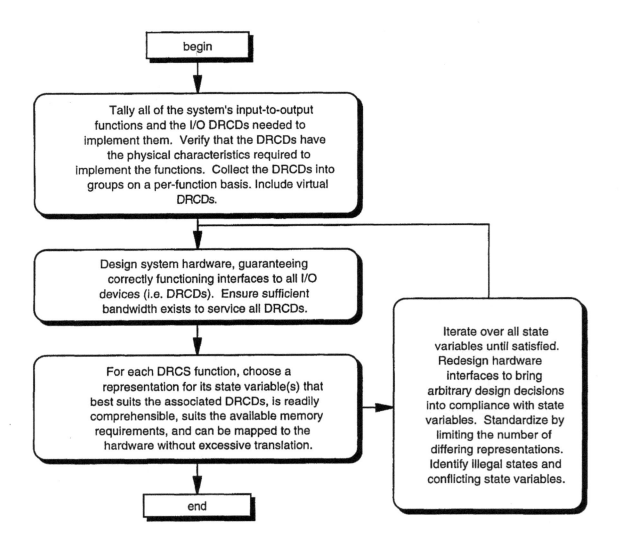

Figure 16: First Phase of DRCS Design Process -- State Variables,
Representations and Harmony with Hardware Design

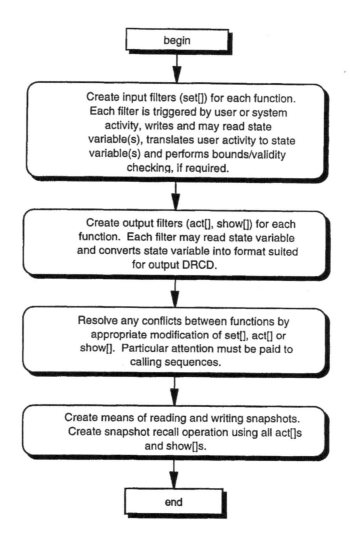

Figure 17: Second Phase of DRCS Design Process -- Filters, Conflict Resolution
and Snapshots

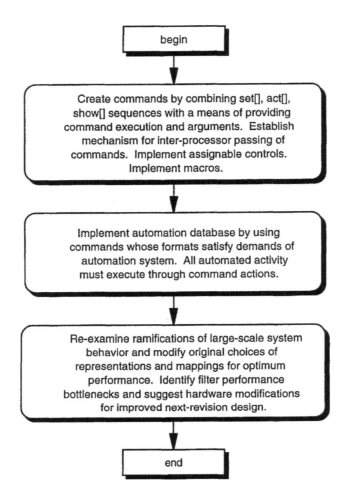

Figure 18: Third Phase of DRCS Design Process -- Commands, Automation and
Large-System Issues

CHAPTER 5
IMPLEMENTATION

The proposed DRCS software was incorporated into a professional audio mixing console according to the guidelines laid out in the previous chapter. The development period was relatively long, which allowed for the trying and rejection of many approaches that were deemed unsatisfactory. In several instances conditions specific to the console's architecture and specifications required enhancements or alterations to the basic scheme. This chapter reviews this implementation of our DRCS software structure.

This professional product, shown in Figure 19, performs amplification, level control, mixing and equalization of analog signals via digital control, and is intended for use in music, live sound, post-production and film work. Typically a single user, the *mix engineer*, operates the console under the direction of one or more clients. The engineer uses his listening skills and mixing abilities to combine the console's audio inputs (live, pre-recorded or synthesized) to create an overall *mix*, typically of two (stereo) or more (e.g. 5.1-channel Dolby® Digital SR-D® for movie theaters [Nor92]) output channels. The console interface is a large surface with knobs, faders, switches and displays. *Mixing* is usually a high-pressure, high-stress environment, with neither room nor time for equipment or operator errors [Hol88]. Large professional consoles cost well in excess of $100,000, so customer expectations of the system's performance and reliability are very high.

Figure 19: The Control (User) Surface of a DRCS-based
Professional Audio Mixing Console

5.1 The Architecture as Implemented

The DRCS software structure was applied to the design of a cost-effective
mixing console with enhanced functionality, reliability, and configurability while
guaranteeing performance regardless of system size. Inexpensive
microprocessors in concert with digitally controllable audio elements formed the
basis of the design. A modular, processor-based design with the DRCS software
structure at its core was the end result. The system consists of four major
hardware components: the *Mix Controller*, the *Audio Mainframe*, the *Patchbay* and
the *Support Computer*. The two units we are concerned with -- the Mix Controller
and the Audio Mainframe -- are highly modular; the console's architecture is

easily expandable and can be configured with anywhere between 8 and 96 faders, in multiples of 8 faders.

The design's power and flexibility lie in the Mix Controller, the "brains" of the system. In normal operation, the Mix Controller monitors the control surface and implements the requisite changes to the audio circuitry in real time (a 1/30s *frame*). The scale of this system[1] quickly overwhelms all but the most powerful single processor's[2] ability to keep up with all the changes that can be made to the control surface in real time (to say nothing of the immense bandwidth required to get all the system signals into and out of the uniprocessor). As a practical example, snapshot recall requires that each I/O channel update 174 bytes in the Audio Mainframe in 1/30 sec. Of course the situation is made increasingly more dire by the expansion of the system through additional channels. The solution is to dedicate a processor to a manageable number of channels, and replicate this as the system grows in size.

Below we present a quick overview of these four major components:

1) The Mix Controller contains from four to fifteen Z80 microprocessors using a shared-memory paradigm to communicate among themselves while running simultaneously and independently. All the DRCS software resides in the Mix Controller; only two of the Z80s are not directly responsible for the system's functions.[3] No audio signals[4] pass through the Mix Controller. Rather, it presents the user with a unique

---

1 A mid-size, 24-channel unit, has 48 faders, 48 microphone preamplifiers, 48 equalizers, 96 auxiliary level sends, 48 mutes, 144 inputs and 120 outputs (I/O), plus 13 inputs and 22 outputs, 2 faders, 14 pots, and 2 mutes (Master). The corresponding stuffing of the Audio Mainframe is 24 I/O Channel modules and one Master Channel module. The system has 38 internal signal busses.

2 A competing, uni-processor product was released at roughly the same time. It failed to gain adherents primarily because of a lack of expandability, and soon vanished.

3 One handles high-speed (>1MBps) communications; the other arbitrates shared memory access, provides synchronization and supports virtual controls.

4 Except the talkback microphone, which must be mounted in the console for convenience.

but recognizable and industry-standard[5] control surface consisting of rotary pots (knobs), linear pots (faders), switches, level meters and illuminated panels to control and display the console's current configuration. The Mix Controller consists of one *Master control module* [6] and up to 12 *I/O control modules*. It has almost negligible power consumption, with its light-emitting diodes (LEDs) responsible for over 80% of the current draw.

2) The Audio Mainframe is a small-refrigerator-sized tower containing all the system's audio-controlling DRCDs. It takes analog input signals and digital control signals and returns analog output signals and digital status signals. The Audio Mainframe consists of a *Master audio module* and up to 28 *I/O audio modules*. Each of the Mix Controller's I/O control modules controls 4 I/O audio modules. The Master audio module and every group of 4 I/O audio modules each have a dedicated bidirectional 1Mbps link to the Mix Controller. The Audio Mainframe consumes approximately 2.5kW in operation.

3) The Patchbay presents the user with an industry-standard means of connecting audio signals to the system -- it's much like an old telephone operator's jack panel. This is a custom, passive, off-the shelf component.

4) The Support Computer, connected to the Mix Controller via a high-speed serial link, provides for off-line (disk) storage of console data, as well as ancillary display functions which require a large, bit-mapped display. It is an extension of the systems UI, to some extent a graphical user interface (GUI). As the GUI developed, so did the link between the Mix Controller and the Support Computer, evolving from a 38.4kbps RS-232 link to a 10Mbps EuBUS connection.[7] The Support Computer is also an off-the shelf component.

---

[5] While the input devices are industry-standard, their arrangement is new and unique to this design.

[6] For packaging and standardization reasons, the Master section (a single Channel, but of a different type) was allocated an entire Z80. It has evolved to the point where its load is approximately equivalent to two I/O channels.

[7] A proprietary point-to-point, bidirectional high-speed link.

The hardware design predated the software by several months, and most of the design was complete before any programming began. A general idea of how many Z80 clock cycles were required to perform the console's functions had been previously established.[8] In order for all these processors to work together, a combination of loosely-coupled and tightly-coupled multiprocessor architectures was developed. In it, each processor spends the vast majority of its time monitoring its own control inputs, effecting changes in the audio circuitry, and displaying the results on the control surface. Of course the user does not want to treat the console as a grouping of independent 4-channel blocks -- rather, the entire control surface should appear transparently as one large, harmonious unit without any physical divisions due to modularity, etc. To this end, a means of intercommunicating between modules was developed, in which several times per frame each processor (and hence each channel, as the processor is the "agent" for up to four channels) can access an area of shared memory, the Bulletin Board, to post & read messages. The code supporting Bulletin Board communications underwent six major revisions in an effort to provide as flexible a messaging scheme in as few clock cycles per processor as was possible.

Many revisions to the specifications and the hardware design were made, some to accommodate desired features in the software. By and large, we were presented with a hardware design that had the perceived ability to execute programs and interface to the DRCDs and to shared memory, with little processing power to spare.

---

[8] The system developed from 4MHz Z80s to 6MHz, and finally to 8MHz parts. A single 16MHz Z180 maintains the 1.25MBps EuBUS connection.

5.2 The Scale of the Problem

To fully appreciate the task that faced the software designers we must examine what had to be done, and how much of it there was to do. First, by examining the partitioning of the console's functions into the I/O and Master control modules, the system's functions are defined. For example, the I/O control module's most basic functionality (per channel) was defined and arranged as:

- 2 19-segment LED meters with programmable ballistics and 16 different modes
- 3 programmable outputs (OUT1-OUT3) using the 6 sources
- other miscellaneous routing and mixing functions
- 2 independent microphone preamps (M1, M2) with 60dB of auto-ranging gain control, phase reverse, high-pass filter and +48V phantom power
- 4 independent auxiliary sends (AUXA-AUXD) with 12-bit level control, 6 sources, 8 destinations, and 34 different modes
- 2 independent fader (UF, LF) with 12-bit level control, 6 sources, 3 (LF) or 27 (UF) destinations, mute and 23 different modes
- 2 independent 4-band parametric equalizers (EQ1, EQ2) with programmable insert points to all 6 sources
- 2 pre- and 2 post-fader SOLOs
- full display of current routing settings via hidden-until-lit LEDs
- positional and clipping LEDs for all pots and faders

This basic I/O functionality was to be repeated for every channel in the console. The Master control module had considerably more such

Figure 20: Console I/O Channel Strip

functionality. The specifications demanded that the system be capable of sustained updates of every single function every 1/30 second. This basic functionality was to be eventually augmented by snapshot recall, automation, grouping and macros, so these higher-level features had to be kept in mind while the system was being designed.

The input DRCDs include momentary pushbutton switches, conventional linear potentiometers sampled by analog-to-digital converters (ADCs), overtemperature sensors, rotary encoders and LEDs packaged in bargraphs, 5x7 character arrays, and individually. The output DRCDs employed include relays,[9] silicon switches,[10] ADCs and digital-to-analog converters (DACs). Very few of the DRCDs support both input and output. The numbers of DRCDs contained in each of the various modules are outlined in Table 10.

Some DRCDs (e.g. 12-bit level attenuators, metering units, equalizer controls) are themselves collections of digitally controlled devices, and are so packaged for various design reasons. A system with 24 channels has input and output DRCDs numbering over five thousand!

5.3 Overview

The design of representations, filters and commands develops roughly concurrently. Once a working model with a few functions is implemented, the designer faces the now rote task of writing the full set of filters and commands for the DRCS. After a basic working system is established, one invariably finds

---

[9] In retrospect, one of the simplest DRCDs.

[10] From which analog multiplexers can be designed.

areas amenable to improved performance. Thereafter, virtually every aspect of the design -- including representations, filters and commands -- must be iterated several times in order to reduce execution times, reduce code size, streamline internal processes and enable new functionality.

Table 10: Console DRCD Count

	Input DRCDs		Output DRCDs	
I/O control module (for 4 channels)	rotary potentiometers	32	bargraph LEDs	152
	linear faders	8	bicolor LEDs	56
	pushbutton switches	60	single-color LEDs	520
	total:	100	total:	728
Master control module	rotary potentiometers	14	bargraph LEDs	152
	linear faders	2	bicolor LEDs	48
	pushbutton switches	100	single-color LEDs	111
	total:	117	5x7 dot-matrix LEDs	24
			total:	335
I/O audio module (1 per channel)	metering units	2	12-bit level attenuators	8
	clip indicators	8	8-bit level attenuators	2
	configuration indicator	1	metering units	2
	total:	11	6-input combiners	14
			equalizer controls	44
			relays	76
			silicon (mute) switches	8
			total:	154
Master audio channel	metering units	8	12-bit level attenuators	24
	clip indicators	10	metering units	8
	total:	18	user bits	4
			relays	51
			silicon switches	28
				115

It is instructive to follow how various issues led to certain design decisions. Instead of attempting to chronicle the development of the hundreds of system functions, as our primary example we will follow a simple function, OUT1, which combines up to six inputs to form a single (mono) output in an I/O channel. Besides the requisite input filter, OUT1 requires two output filters --

one for the control DRCD, and one for the UI DRCD. The development of this function is representative of the effort required to complete the system.

5.4 Standardized Representations

The OUT1 function is quite straightforward, in that it controls the state of six independent bipolar solid-state switches. Additionally, six LEDs corresponding to the six switches present the state of OUT1 to the user. The situation for other functions was similar; the polarity of the solid-state switches and relays was not overwhelmingly standardized, but the polarities of the LEDs usually were -- a 0 meant that the LED was on, a 1 that the LED was off (active low). Despite the hardware's bias towards an active-low representation, we discovered that active-high was easier to explain to programmers and sophisticated users who created their own macros. This led to an important decision concerning representations -- that all switch-type functions in the console would be active high in their state variables. This meant that some translation would be required when reflecting the state of the function in the UI. In those DRCDs that were not active low, a simple toggle operation was all that was required, and this was shown to have a negligible effect on the system's performance (see below). Additionally, it meant that all instances of virtual controllers that dealt with switch-type functions could treat the data in the same way, eliminating any extra coding to handle one of two possible polarities.

Due to the Z80's poor performance in bit-oriented instructions and due to real-world memory constraints, it is undesirable to dedicate individual memory locations (bytes) to each DRCS function. Rather, we collect DRCS functions in groups (or *blocks*) that corresponded to the presentation on the surface of the Mix Controller. Instead of having six state variables to represent the current settings of the six silicon switches in OUT1, all six bits are collected into a single byte to form a state variable for the OUT1 meta-function. Wherever possible the bits are arranged to correspond to the bit alignment of the actual hardware.

5.5 Input Filters

The large number of DRCDs and the repetitiveness of the functions they performed would quickly have led to large and unmanageable code if the filters were not standardized. Input filters were invariably the simplest, especially when the associated function had only a virtual (assignable) control. In these cases the function is controlled through the execution of a command. OUT1's input filter simply limits the allowable value of the command's argument, masking out any unused and/or potentially dangerous bits, and then writes a new byte-sized value to the state variable:

```
set_OUT_1_src:      and     00111111b
                    _wr_Snapshot_byte   OUT_1_src
                    ret
```

where OUT_1_src is an index into the channel's current snapshot. The new value for OUT1 is carried implicitly in the Z80's A register. This input filter is a simple assembly-language subroutine of a few bytes, and differs from the input filters for OUT2 and OUT3 by only a single piece of information, the state variable index:

```
set_OUT_2_src:      and     00111111b
                    _wr_Snapshot_byte   OUT_2_src
                    ret
set_OUT_3_src:      and     00111111b
                    _wr_Snapshot_byte   OUT_3_src
                    ret
```

So as not to lose sight of the advantage of this state-variable-based scheme, note that if this system were coded in a high-level language, these three functions would reduce to:

```
set_OUT_1_src:      set_6bit_src (new_val, OUT_1_src);
set_OUT_2_src:      set_6bit_src (new_val, OUT_2_src);
set_OUT_3_src:      set_6bit_src (new_val, OUT_3_src);
```

with improved legibility and potential savings in source code size.

5.6 State Variables and Snapshots

Due to limits on available memory, some systems may require that the amount of memory allocated to snapshots be minimized. Others, with high communications bandwidth and lots of available memory, can accommodate large snapshots without difficulty. What the state variables represent often affects how they are stored in memory. We found that access to the state variables -- whether one at a time or via an entire snapshot -- is the defining issue for the arrangement of state variables in the current snapshot.

In a system where code and data memory are physically separate and data memory is at a premium, it is beneficial to pack the state variables into memory as densely as possible or to use as few state variables as possible. Code is then used to extract and/or transform the state variable information into a format more suitable for the output filters. This extraction/transformation is costly in terms of execution cycles consumed and memory required. The designer must balance the advantages of a minimal set of state variables against the loss in performance due to the corresponding housekeeping. This is where the tradeoff between data memory and code memory of a segmented architecture occurs.

The solution -- a win-win situation as long as there is sufficient memory available -- is to analyze the frequency-of-use of each state variable and store it within the snapshot in a format that requires the least overhead when interfacing to the input and output filters. If the number of format conversions for a given state variable exceeds some threshold, then the original choice of state variable representation was unfortunate, or additional state variables are needed for the particular function. This is not unreasonable, as the state variables themselves are very small,[11] and hence the designer is afforded much latitude. It is the number of state variables, particularly those associated with a particular function, that must be examined.

For example, two input devices may be stored as low-resolution positional state variables, and are transformed through a lengthy process to higher-resolution formats suitable for additional processing with a third input. If the third input is constantly changing, it will be necessary to continually perform the same low-to-high-resolution transformation on all three, always yielding the same interim result for the first two. This is highly inefficient. If however, we automatically store the high-resolution data as a state variable alongside the positional ones, then we have completely removed the cost in execution time associated with the unchanging inputs. While this does not minimize the code size, it completely removes redundant execution, at the cost of a few bytes of snapshot memory.

The result is a snapshot structure that contains multiple state variables associated with particular DRCDs. This is also driven by the need for different functions utilizing the same output DRCDs. For example, the user can operate the level controlling elements (a pair of rotary and linear potentiometers) of a

---

[11] Their size is tied to their resolution, which for a variety of reasons (human perception, physical devices, etc.) rarely exceeds 24 bits.

fader block in twelve different *modes.* Five of the most commonly used modes, and the corresponding functions of the input devices, are represented below. In each mode the user is controlling the contribution of one or more signal sources to the left and right (output) channels. The functions of the pot and fader change from mode to mode, as does the steering of the signal sources -- in stereo, the signal sources remain independent and do not mix, whereas in mono they are all summed together and then distributed to the left and right channels.

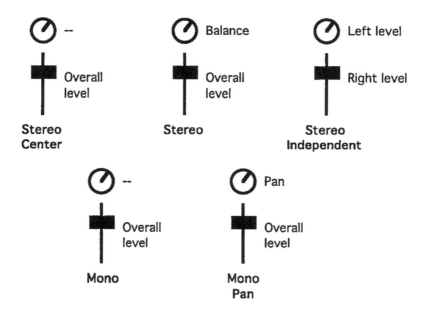

Figure 21: Multiple Operating Modes Using Two Input
DRCDs

By choosing to treat each of these modes (represented by the *mode* state variable) as unique console functions, we can enhance the console's performance by removing all repetitive position-to-level computations. In this case, five different state variables were assigned to the fader block, of which each mode uses one or two:

Table 11: Fader Block Modes and their State Variables

Mode	State Variable(s)
Stereo Center	center_level
Stereo	center_level, balance
Stereo Independent	left_level, right_level
Mono	center_level
Mono Pan	center_level, pan

The penalty for failing to eliminate unnecessary computations in a large DRCS can be quite high. This improvement was absolutely necessary to enable the *Grouping* function, in which the overall level of the fader block is adjusted up or down by a *Master* fader. Without it, each movement of the Master fader of a large group of faders consumed nearly 20% of the console's overall processing power (per frame). With the multi-state-variable scheme in place, the load was undetectable.

The context of the fader block, described by the mode state variable, dictates which of these state variables is linked to the user input, and how they are combined to form the control words for the fader block DRCDs. Two additional state variables, *upper_position* and *lower_position*, are used to track the actual positions of the knob and fader. Maintaining two or more simultaneous representations (one for the function, the other for the user interface) improves execution speed in other time-critical operations like snapshot recall and automation playback, usually by avoiding processor-intensive computational translations.

Often the need for these optimizations only becomes apparent once the system had been operating for some time. Snapshot size grows in order to support all these state variables, as does the number of commands in the system. Snapshot recall is unaffected by the use of additional state variables.

Even with an increased number of state variables used, the actual number of representations should be kept to a minimum. In both the I/O and the Master modules, the representations were:

Table 12: State Variable Representations Used

Representation	Used by	Format
level, balance	faders auxiliaries microphones equalizers oscillator	signed, 12-bit, covering a range of 72.25dB with increments of 1/32dB
pan	faders auxiliaries	signed, 8-bit, covering a range of 180 degrees in increments of 1 degree
switches	inputs assignments outputs mutes	1-bit (0: off, 1: on), often grouped into bytes according to block's function
frequency	equalizers oscillator	8-bit, covering a range of discrete logarithmic frequencies from 20.6Hz to 21.1kHz
Q (i.e. 1/bandwidth)	equalizers	8-bit, covering a range of discrete values from 0.32 to 11.6

The use of table lookup is advantageous wherever console functions require a non-linear translation between user input and the corresponding state variable. For example, each of the 256 possible positions of a level-controlling fader correspond to a predetermined, not necessarily linear, signal attenuation. By using a table, the relatively low-resolution 8-bit positional information is readily converted to a 12-bit level state variable. Recently, table-lookup-and-interpolate instructions have become available in some processors [Mot90].

Code size will be minimized by choosing fewer representations and optimizing the routines to convert one into another. For example, a single routine can perform all additions involving levels (in dB), while another displays levels in dB on the Master control panel's alphanumeric display, regardless of the source of the data. The use of standardized representations helps greatly in resolving problems and minimizes debugging effort. The physical size of state variables (e.g. 8 or 16 bits long) should match the design's architecture and the processor's abilities. There is little reason to compact memory allocated to sparsely-filled state variables if the chosen processor cannot not do this efficiently.

Another issue that relates to state variables is the case where a function is governed primarily by a clearly identifiable input device, but a large number of secondary actions or settings affect it, too. These functions are usually described *in toto* as the logical combination of many inputs. Attempting to modify such a function can rapidly cause headaches. The solution is particularly elegant -- to combine the state of all the inputs to the function into a single, multi-bit number. This state variable is then passed onto the output filters to effect the requisite changes. That the state of the function is defined by data, and not code, is key to this method. By investing in pre-processing code to create the state variable, the output filters are kept especially simple and fast.

5.7 Output Filters

OUT1's control DRCD bits are active low, so OUT1's output filter must complement the state variable before transferring it to the DRCD:

```
act_OUT_1_src:
act_OUT_2_src:      call   rd_AM_block_ptr
```

```
ld      (IX+AM_STEERING_BYTE),AM_STEER_SRC_1_2
_rd_Snapshot_byte   OUT_1_src
cpl
ld      (IX+AM_DATA_BYTE1),A
_rd_Snapshot_byte   OUT_2_src
cpl
ld      (IX+AM_DATA_BYTE2),A
call    save_new_AM_block
ret
```

This filter is called without any arguments. For performance reasons, control data to the output DRCDs was buffered, and then sent to the Audio Mainframe all at once, once per frame. In cases like this, where the hardware design allowed the sharing of a 16-bit control word by OUT1 and OUT2, $act\_OUT\_1\_src$ and $act\_OUT\_2\_src$ were identical. This had the benefit that only a single call had to be made during snapshot recall to handle the control DRCD updates for OUT1 and OUT2, but had the disadvantage that commands to both functions within the same update period would require twice the control data bandwidth than was absolutely necessary.[12] If this were a critical issue, a different means of updating the DRCDs could be developed.

The two cpl (one's complement) operations in $act\_OUT\_1\_src$ account for only 8 of 258 clock cycles (3%), and only 2 of 30 bytes (6%) of code memory used. Standardization and understandability that accompany a chosen representation (in this case active-high) greatly outweigh the disadvantages of these mild increases in execution time and memory requirements. Similarly, in all other output filters simple format changes between the state variables and the DRCDs achieve the same unification.

In $act\_OUT\_1\_src$, no attempt is made to control the upper two bits that are sent to OUT1's DRCD. Such a precaution would be wasteful of computing

---

[12] This also results in a reduction in code size due to the system's hardware design, and not due to any issues of software organization.

power, as the bits are unused in the hardware. The precaution was, however, necessary when storing the state variable, for other parts of the system depended on the unused bits in the state variable being set to 0. This decision to guarantee the value of unused bits proved to be a good one, as many functions that interacted with such state variables could be simplified by the removal of extra bit-masking operations.

The control DRCD hardware for OUT1 is shown schematically in Figure 23 (see Appendix E).

OUT1's UI DRCD bits are also active low, so *show_OUT_1_src* also requires a complement operation. Due to the arrangement of OUT1's LEDs the function is considerably more complex, as listed below:

```
show_OUT_1_src:    ld      DE,mp_LEDs_ptr
                   call    rd_Channel_word
                   ld      (mp_LED_SR_ptr),DE
                   ld      DE,OUT1_mp_LEDs
                   ld      HL,(base_Ch_dat)
                   add     HL,DE
                   ld      (mp_LED_ctrl_tbl_ptr),HL
                   _rd_Snapshot_byte   OUT_1_src
                   cpl
                   ld      C,A
                   call    show_OUT
                   ret
```

This filter also has no arguments, as it operates implicitly on the state variable *OUT_1_src*. Once the filter was written and proven to work correctly, its apparent complexity was hidden from the programmer. Once shown to work correctly, output filters can often be substantially optimized for speed, thus improving system performance in a myriad of operating conditions, including command execution, snapshot recall and automation. *Show_OUT_2_src* and *show_OUT_3_src* are, of course, identical except for references to state variables and some pointers. The lack of a rich set of Z80 registers precluded a more passed-parameter-based format for many filters. The UI DRCD hardware for OUT1 is shown schematically in Figure 24 (see Appendix E).

This example illustrates how the DRCS structure, with its input and output filters, can easily adapt to machine limitations. To make use of a physical device connected to the system, only the creation of software to translate the state variable to control data suitable to the device is required. This is often trivial. Regardless of the complexity of the DRCD interface, the filter alone contains DRCD-specific code. The representation of the associated state variable(s) can be as arbitrary as necessary with respect to the physical device. Hence the designer is free to concentrate on which state variable representations suit his purposes best, and can generally neglect the device-specific attributes of the DRCDs. However, a balance should be struck between the elegance of a particular state variable representation and the benefits of reducing the number of translations between formats. A particular representation may simplify the output filter for an indicator tremendously, but may complicate the filter for an actuator. Should changes to a filter be necessary, for example due to hardware upgrades, the effect will be localized to the filter and will not propagate through the rest of the system. A modular hardware design is thus complemented by a modular software design via the DRCS structure.

5.8 Commands

A few hundred commands are required to support the preponderance of assignable controls on the user interface surface of the Mix Controller. Overhead associated with command execution is detrimental to system performance, as it is repeatedly invoked through normal operation, automated operation, and the execution of macros. Choosing a single, unified command structure with a single entry point will minimize code requirements and make optimization easier. As mentioned in Chapter 4, the command format must contain enough unambiguous data to uniquely specify the desired action of any function in the DRCS. The specification of this format may be highly dependent on other aspects of the design, including the means of inter-processor communications and external communications interfaces.

The DRCS software structure defines commands as set[], act[], show[] sequences. While commands can be written as in-line code, instead of a sequence of subroutines, the penalty associated with doing so is very low. Additionally, since act[] and show[] are used elsewhere, this actually minimizes memory requirements. For example, the OUT1 command was of the form:

```
cmd_OUT_1_src:      call    set_OUT_1_src
                    call    act_OUT_1_src
                    jp13    show_OUT_1_src
```

Once again, the new value for OUT1 is carried implicitly in the 8-bit A register, so the command has a single 8-bit argument. Commands requiring 16-bit arguments (the practical upper limit for a design based on Z80 processors) would pass their values to the command in a 16-bit register. This command format used two 8-bit arguments -- in OUT1's case the second 8-bit argument is unused. The overhead incurred by forming the command from three separate filters remains under 1% for both speed and code size (see Appendix D).

Simple input filters, where the command's argument overwrites the current state variable, may be adequate for all console functionality, including automation. However, the introduction of macros places new demands on the

---

[13] A `call qqqq, ret` sequence at the end of any function can be replaced by `jp qqqq` with savings of 1 byte and 10 clock cycles.

console. From the user's perspective, it should be possible to change each part of a switch-type function individually without affecting the other parts. Simple input filters prevent the command structure from supporting this type of functionality for macros, as *a priori* knowledge of the value of the state variable is required to change individual bits when the command can only overwrite the entire state variable. Normally, extra memory storage or bandwidth dedicated to providing this information would be necessary. However, as the DRCS is command-driven, it is simple to augment certain commands to support this functionality without altering the basic set[], act[], show[] command paradigm.

The solution is a "pre-processor" to the input filters of switch-type commands, which gives such commands the ability to manipulate as few or as many bits as desired without affecting the others. This pre-processor supports the ability to set (1), clear (0) or toggle any combination of individual bits, and the ability to set, clear or write all the bits in the state variable. This required the use of two command arguments, where the first indicates what kind of operation is desired (*ON, OFF, TGL, SET, CLR, WR*), and the second is a bit pattern corresponding to the bits to be changed in the state variable. The command then looks like this:

```
cmd_OUT_1_src:    _rtn_Prop_Mod_svar_arg   OUT_1_src
                  call    set_OUT_1_src
                  call    act_OUT_1_src
                  jp      show_OUT_1_src
```

and the command syntax (in pseudocode) to turn send microphone inputs M1 and M2 out OUT1 without changing the status of its inputs L1 through L4 is:

```
cmd_OUT_1_src (ON, 00000011b);
```

_Rtn_Prop_Mod_svar_arg uses the bit pattern as a mask to protect the state variable bits that are to remain unchanged, and to alter (in this case, make active) the bits specified by the command's second argument. The addition of this preprocessor to the switch-type commands enhances the utility of macros, simplifies the coding of the user interface for switch-type function and reduces the bandwidth requirements between the assignable controls and these functions. Switch-type functions can now be directly changed instead of through a read-modify-write arrangement. This comes at the cost of a single additional subroutine, resulting in no more than an additional 5% execution time per switch command (see Appendix D).

The situation above illustrates the difficulty in optimally organizing a DRCS's functions -- any attempt to group individual DRCDs into functional blocks with a single command will result in a tradeoff between memory economies to support the function and control over each individual DRCD. OUT1's six 1-bit DRCDs could have been assigned to six individual commands and state variables, simplifying the filters involved and improving execution speeds. However, considerably more code and data memory would be consumed. This is especially apparent wherever assignable controls are involved. The choice of 8- or 16-bit processors may dictate that one design for byte- or word-sized state variables, which reduces the number of state variables and commands, but makes it more difficult to control single-bit DRCS functions. Functions that require inseparable multi-bit state variables for multi-bit DRCDs (e.g. multi-bit level controllers) do not suffer from these problems.

The I/O channels have 86 commands that operate directly on state variables, and another 52 that perform higher-level (e.g. snapshot recall, grouping, automation control) and systems-level (e.g. restart) commands. The corresponding numbers for the Master module are 51 and 29. The commands and their filters represent roughly 40%, or 25KB, of each module's code space. The utility of a standardized scheme becomes apparent with such a large investment in programming effort -- for example, the repetitive structure of the commands allows the use of automated programming tools to edit the commands *en masse* if a particular change or code optimization is desired. For blocks of repeated, identical functions, the respective commands differ only in their references to state variables and physical constants associated with their DRCDs. Also, the predictable behavior of all the DRCS function commands means that the performance improvements of such code optimizations can be accurately predicted.

As the number of DRCS functions increases, commands play an ever-more-important role in implementing them. In its final incarnation, the messaging scheme allowed any channel to send messages to any other channel of up to 16K bytes in length (complete with a notification of the sender), and the total number of messages was controlled only by the space available on the Bulletin Board (30KB). The need for a more flexible command format was driven by issues outside the scope of the DRCS's basic functionality. The additional bytes required by the new commands simplified many internal console functions, but the overhead involved led to some important changes to the Automation system (see below).

5.8.1 Implementing Automation

A description of the advantages of automation in mixing consoles illustrates the importance of a DRCS structure that is amenable to automation:

> Today, when working on an automated console, a recording engineer begins a stereo mixdown by playing the multitrack master tape and adjusting fader knobs up and down just as he had in the past. However, the mixing done on the faders by the engineer is "remembered" by the console's central processing unit (CPU). After the song has been played

through and mixed, the engineer can rewind the tape and play it back, and all the faders levels he mixed are automatically reproduced including all static and changing levels. It is then a relatively simple matter for the engineer to continue to go back and do additional mixing as necessary without having to redo all of the work he had done previously. It also makes the refining of a complex production requiring twenty, thirty or more mix passes immensely easier. The vast majority of mixing decisions from previous mix passes that were satisfactory continue to be reproduced automatically, while the engineer can concentrate on subtler and subtler refinements. This technology, in large part, makes possible the high quality, state-of-the-art recordings and soundtracks heard today. [Pet93, p. 7-8]

The early implementations of automation focused on storing commands with state-variable arguments. This was in part due to a desire to be able to visualize the operation of the console from the database, and also due to the limited amount of processing power afforded outside the scope of the Mix Controller. Since each stored command unambiguously contains the time-stamped value of its corresponding DRCS function, it is easiest to simply take the commands resulting from user actions and store them immediately into the automation database. In this implementation the database and all automation operations were local to each channel. As long as the command format contains only the information required to playback the user's actions, this scheme remains a viable one. This results in the especially elegant situation where all activity in the console is of the same format, and is readily recognized by any sort of viewer.

We found, however, a disadvantage to this scheme; namely, that users perceive their actions in terms of their use of the controls, not the effect of the controls. In other words, when reviewing automation they were solely concerned with the activities of the surface of the console, and not what was occurring underneath. This is an important distinction. For example, in order to smoothly re-record a fader's moves in an automation pass, the beginning and ending levels must match those of the previous pass to avoid any unwanted jumps in audible level. These two level-matching points (in time) are called the *punch-in* and *punch-out* points, and visual indicators, so-called *align LEDs*,[14] are usually provided to constantly compare the positional status of the currently recorded moves against the previous values. The user pays careful attention to these indicators during punch-in and punch-out. The indicator values for the current position are derived from positional DRCD information, and the values for the previous (i.e. currently being replayed) values are derived from the state variables in the automation file. Note that these two data do not necessarily map one-to-one, especially in the case of continuous controllers.

The difficulty in displaying meaningful alignment information grows as additional user inputs are combined simultaneously. The solution is to make all alignment comparisons based on the same type of data. This is accomplished by the function $f^{-1}[]$ described in Chapter 4, which transforms state variable data back to positional information. Without this standardization the unavoidable ambiguity of this level-controller mapping led to user complaints of a perceived lack of repeatability when (re-) positioning unlocked controls after snapshot recall or during automation.

It is instructive to review the strength of the DRCS structure in light of demands placed on the console by the automation system that exceeded the processing capacity and communications bandwidth of the original design. As the demand for new console-wide automation functions forced the command packet to grow from a constant 6 bytes to a variable-length scheme with a minimum of 14 bytes, the extra command overhead began to take an unacceptable toll on automated performance. Eventually the limited power of

---

[14] These are illustrated in Figure 25 (see Appendix E) as they appear on the surface of the console. There are three LEDs, and all are off if the fader is locked. When unlocked, either a red "up arrow, " a red "down arrow " or a green "on-target" LED is illuminated.

the Mix Controller's processors and programming environment could not support the further evolution of the Crescendo's automation system, and these functions were assigned to the Support Computer. This was made possible by the addition of a very-high-speed bidirectional communications link between the console and the Support Computer.

The decision to implement automation in this way was due to several reasons: an abundance of high-level programming experience on larger computers than the DRCS itself, a lack of expandability in the DRCS computer hardware (we had reached the limit in memory space and processor speed), the need to manage very large databases, and the suitability of the PC to the task at hand. The previous state-variable-based automation system was deemed unsuitable to this arrangement, primarily because of the high bandwidth required to move commands between the Mix Controller and the Support Computer. This new automation system was also built entirely around the Support Computer's UI, and made no attempt to extract or display any information outside of the console's UI.

It is notable that despite this complete turnabout in the design and operation of the automation system, extremely little programming had to be done to accommodate the new automation. To the contrary, the DRCS scheme allowed for a very easy integration of the advanced automation facility into the system as a whole, and required very few changes to the underlying structure. Apart from removing all the previous automation-management code (essentially large-linked-list management), only a means of redirecting user activity either into the system or through the Support Computer was required (see Figure 22). This was possible because user activity forms the input to the DRCS's input filters. Capturing these actions before they reached the input filters could be accomplished unbeknownst to the rest of the system. The resulting automation database contains minimum-sized records of new user input values and input DRCD indices, and operates solely on this information. Separating the development of the automation system from the development of the DRCS has been a great success.

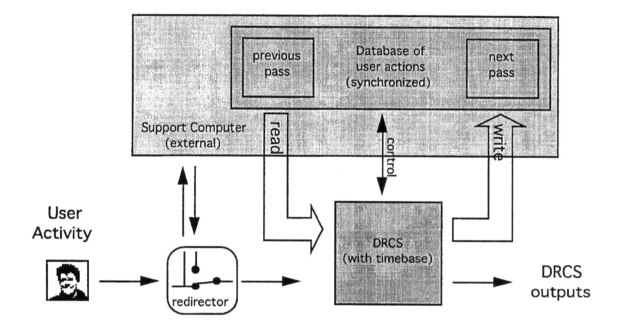

Figure 22: Automated Operation with External Computer
(shown with user activity redirection bypassed)

5.9 Other Difficulties

The process outlined in Chapter 4 allows the tackling of the problems of conflicting DRCD settings (see Appendix A) and arbitrary hardware design decisions (see Appendix C). These problems were solved without compromising the basic tenets of our software structure. Additionally, some mismatches between state variable formats and DRCD bit patterns were unavoidable, and "converters" for certain output filters had to be written. Fortunately these converters never involved more than byte-sized bit transformations, so they were easy to optimize for execution speed and/or memory requirements.

For example, the density of some indicator LEDs (packed on a 0.200" x 0.500" grid), coupled with the requirement that the printed-circuit board be of conventional manufacture with two routing layers and conservative trace widths, did not allow for the control signals to be routed in such a way that their order on the signal bus corresponded to their ordering in the corresponding state variable. This same ordering was applied to the control DRCDs for similar reasons. Schematics for the control and UI DRCDs for OUT1 are shown in Figures 25 and 26, respectively (see Appendix E). This semi-arbitrary decision arose because of real-world cost constraints. The solution is to provide a bit-translator in act[] and show[] to accommodate this limitation of the physical hardware. Should this design artifact be removed in later hardware revisions, then the translator would become unnecessary.

Table 13: State-Variable-to-LED Translation Table

State Variable	Bus Signal	Indicator LED
bit 0 - MT1	MT_LED_0	"1"
bit 1 - MT2	MT_LED_7	"2"
bit 2 - MT3	MT_LED_1	"3"
bit 3 - MT4	MT_LED_6	"4"
bit 4 - MT5	MT_LED_2	"5"
bit 5 - MT6	MT_LED_5	"6"
bit 6 - MT7	MT_LED_3	"7"
bit 7 - MT8	MT_LED_4	"8"

The code to effect this transformation is shown below, and is called within the show[] routines for the Upper Fader Multitrack Assigns. This routine requires less memory (52 bytes) than, but is not as fast as, a routine that would use a 256-

byte lookup table to effect the translation. The ease of adding such routines to filters allows the designer to optimize the filter as needed.

```
xlator:      ld    B,A
             ld    A,11111111b      ; assume all OFF
             bit   0,B              ; b0 <-> b0
             jr    NZ,xlator_1
             res   0,A
xlator_1:    bit   1,B              ; b1 <-> b7
             jr    NZ,xlator_2
             res   7,A
xlator_2:    bit   2,B              ; b2 <-> b1
             jr    NZ,xlator_3
             res   1,A
xlator_3:    bit   3,B              ; b3 <-> b6
             jr    NZ,xlator_4
             res   6,A
xlator_4:    bit   4,B              ; b4 <-> b2
             jr    NZ,xlator_5
             res   2,A
xlator_5:    bit   5,B              ; b5 <-> b5
             jr    NZ,xlator_6
             res   5,A
xlator_6:    bit   6,B              ; b6 <-> b3
             jr    NZ,xlator_7
             res   3,A
xlator_7:    bit   7,B              ; b7 <-> b4
             jr    NZ,xlator_8
             res   4,A
xlator_8:    ret
```

Whereas the translator for the control and UI DRCDs of the first eight multitrack assigns are identical, those for the latter 16 are not. They are, however, very similar to *xlator*. *Xlator's* use is illustrated below:

```
show_UF_mt1_asgn:    _rd_Snapshot_byte   UF_mt1_asgn
                     cpl
                     call   xlator
                     ld     DE,cp_LEds+9
                     jp     wr_Channel_byte
```

5.10 Alternative DRCD Implementations

Coding any large problem can be met with a seemingly near-endless variety of alternative coding methodologies.

> Although a computer is a precise instrument designed to execute a finite set of instructions, it is also very flexible, allowing innumerable combinations of individual instructions to accomplish the same task. [Pri88, p. 142]

In the case of the DRCS, it is instructive to discuss alternatives to a state-variable-based approach. While we cannot possibly list all alternate approaches, we can review a few. Many intellectually "elegant" approaches using less well-known programming languages and computer hardware are the most difficult to address, as there are few experts and not many experienced programmers:

> Have you ever noticed that there are no intermediate Forth programmers? You are either a rank beginner or a black-belt guru ... the source code of a professional Forth system is likely to be tightly packed, handcoded, over-optimized, and generally incomprehensible. [Tra90, p. 38]

The general programming public's aversion to these outspoken advocates' programming environments has led many of the protagonists to meticulously document and benchmark their work in an effort to win over possible converts. This is a very hotly contested area, one difficult to review. An alternative scheme from this body of programming knowledge would probably bring with it good, hard quantitative data as to its efficiency, speed, etc.

A simple alternative, perhaps one that an unseasoned programmer might attempt, would be to single-thread all the DRCS functions (i.e. create in-line code) from input to output, and perhaps contain them all in the case of snapshot recall. However, it should be clear that the breaking up of the single thread into set[], act[] and show[] suffers only the penalty of additional calling and loading overhead (i.e. speed) and a few bytes of code memory. This is minor (as shown previously), and is more than offset by increased readability and modularity. By destroying the minimal connectedness of the filters, the maintenance, extendibility and reusability suffer greatly. The very minor optimizations in speed and size that are gained through in-line code are best avoided or only applied when the design has reached full maturity and will no longer evolve.

Obviously many tricks can be employed to speed up performance -- for example any processor/compiler that could keep state variables in registers instead of in memory could gain both speed (fewer memory operations) and flexibility (extended register operations typical of these architectures).

Lastly, one can almost always trade more memory for increased speed. This would be accompanied by simultaneously storing variables for all three levels (user input, state variable (in a standardized format) and physical layer (DRCD native representation)). In this manner there is no need for act[] to do the necessary translations for snapshot recall, and in fact all the physical layer variables can be pre-formatted for transfer to the DRCDs. Juggling simultaneous equivalent representations proves to be difficult because of a lack of strictly 1-to-1 mapping, greatly increases memory, code size and processor power requirements, and often results in redundant data storage. In absolutely time-critical applications, however there may be substantial benefits to be gained by not having to translate between formats. All of these suggestions should be viewed as optimizations to a basic software structure. They restrict the flexibility of the underlying scheme, but may be necessary (and perhaps cost-effective) in certain cases.

5.11 Analysis

We have proposed a method for structuring software in the DRCS, and via its application we have created a working, large-scale system. In the previous sections we have individually outlined the benefits, disadvantages and costs of the various software components that together comprise our complete approach to DRCS programming. Now we must assess these same qualities -- as well as the issue of reliability -- of the method as a whole, as well as of the resulting system. Many of these issues are interrelated.

5.11.1 Costs of Method

The costs associated with the application of our software structure to a DRCS include the actual cost of coding, the cost in verifying the correctness of the implementation and the costs of testing and maintenance. The simplicity (or "tightness") of the code does much to reduce the cost, as the net result is a very regular and repeated structure for all the elements in our scheme. We have found that through examples and brief instruction new programmers have quickly become proficient in creating new DRCS functions with the attendant filters, state variables and commands. The visibility of each function's status through its state variable reduces the need for debugging aids and the subsequent lost time when debugging the system. Correctness has been easy to verify through the straightforward and testable behavior of each of the filters. Testing and maintenance costs are decreased for the same reasons, as each function can be exercised on an individual basis to verify correctness. When coding new functions from scratch, we have found that a programmer's most common stumbling block revolves around the choice of representation for the state variable, if for no other reason that this is where considerable design latitude exists. This methodology has an inherently low programming cost primarily due to its simplified and standardized design, the hierarchical organization of it basic elements and the ability to develop DRCS functions in isolation from the rest of the system software.

5.11.2 Reliability of Method

In terms of assessing the reliability of our method, we define the system as the actions and results of the programmer following our prescribed methodology to create a DRCS. The reliability of any system can be defined as the probability that it will perform in its intended purpose for a specified time under stated conditions of use [Pri88]. With software, "the key contributor to reliability is precise design," and unreliability is attributable to design errors [Mye76, p. 4]. After all, software itself does not wear out. The reliability of our system, i.e. how well it is designed and the measure of how reliably it can be applied to other systems, is greatly dependent on the accuracy and completeness of its specifications. Our specifications encompass all the issues that must be resolved for a set of DRCS input-to-output functions to work correctly, from the hardware design stage all the way to system operations with higher-level functionality.

Fault *avoidance, detection, correction* and *tolerance* are the four approaches to software reliability [Mye76]. In our method, fault avoidance is achieved through the choice of appropriate representations, followed by the creation of verifiably correct input and output filters to act on state variables in the chosen representation. These filters are then tied together in a specified sequence to form commands. Fault detection and correction for our method involves reviewing (either manually or automatically) each state variable, filter and command to ensure that some rudimentary procedures (filter correctness, rules for modifying state variables, sequencing, etc.) are observed. The issue of fault tolerance is not applicable to our system, except that an automated system could employ a self-check to find violations of the basic tenets of our methodology.

Exposure of the results of our method to wholly new environments (e.g. higher-level programming, substantially-altered system requirements) have, after analysis, not required any modifications to our method.

5.11.3 Benefits of Method

The cost and reliability issues concerning our method all point out that its primary benefit is the simplicity of its application. To successfully employ our method, the DRCS programmer must be familiar with digital remotely controlled devices and must master three basic concepts -- filters, state variables and commands. Only a knowledge of the device characteristics and the user interface is necessary to fully specify these software constructs. The choice of programming language is immaterial. To code them is demonstrably simple and straightforward. Where non-trivial complications arise we have proposed relatively simple solutions which maintain the integrity of the method. The links between our software structures are straightforward and are transparent to the overall workings of the system. Our structures completely define and execute the input-to-output chain of control and the feedback of information to the user. Our functions can be made to handle, without error, the complete range of user input activity.

Our method presents, in a guide form, a "cradle-to-grave" approach to writing software for digital remotely-controlled systems. By following our methodology the somewhat burdensome (because of scale and repetition) task of getting the basic DRCS "up and running" is substantially reduced, hence quickening the pace of system development. Our method is totally independent of hardware details, and remains applicable to a design over its entire lifespan. Once in place, the DRCS functions will perform reliably and deterministically, freeing the programmer for other tasks.

5.11.4 Disadvantages of Method

Our method has a few disadvantages, none of them serious. While comprehension of the individual elements of our approach is often quickly achieved, an appreciation for why they are structured this way often eludes the programmer until the system is ready for higher-level functionality. Our focus has been to present a method that delivers working code for the DRCS. Both the method and the resultant code have been fine-tuned, but not at the expense of optimizing one over the other. This suggests that there are still areas where the programming effort could be reduced. It is conceivable that an automated system could be designed, which took as its inputs the details of the DRCDs and the user's perception of the system, and produced as its output complete state variables specifications, filters and commands in the language of choice. It is difficult to be more specific about the choice of representations, as hardware technology is constantly changing and a formalized approach to quantifying user perceptions requires human factors research. There may also be advantages to indexing the command structure directly to the state variables -- this is a subject of ongoing research [Kal93].

5.11.5 Costs of Implementation

The costs of applying this software method to our implementation have been very low. While building the system, creation of the scheme's basic elements was observed to be fast and nearly error free. The simplicity of the filters lends itself well to bottom-up testing, speeding up development by allowing the programmers to mark portions of the design as "verifiably correct." Education of new programmers to become proficient in our method has been quick and easy. While writing the DRCS software the highest-cost activities (as measured by the programmer's reluctance to embark on them and the subsequent time spent) have been follow-on reviews of all the filters to ensure bounds checking, correction of user input and that no operations were being spent on unneeded masking of bit-based functions.

The hardware costs associated with fitting this method into our implementation have not been without controversy. While there is agreement that the filters provide an excellent balance of code size vs. speed of execution, there have been several instances where choices of representation[15] and command-argument formats have come under attack. Regardless, the regular structure of the system's code has made the desired changes straightforward. The costs associated with testing, inspecting, maintaining and supporting the function code in this large DRCS have been minimal, thus achieving quality at low cost. At this point the amount of memory and processor power dedicated to

---

[15] For example, a representation based on 1/10dB steps is now considered more appropriate for the console, as this resolution is more commonly found in audio measurements, primarily due to the test equipment used. The choice of the wrong representation may even compromise the products presentation -- in this instance some specifications (e.g. gain accuracy) would be improved through the use of the 1/10dB format for audio levels.

providing the DRCS with its I/O functions is considered acceptable and probably optimal for our implementation.

It is instructive to review replacement costs. Motorola has issued an application note [Mot82] which described their Z80-to-68000 cross-assembler and its performance. The 68000 is a later-generation processor with a 16-/32-bit architecture and a much larger set of registers. Where the Z80 has been successful in embedded designs, the 68k series has done well in general-purpose computers and as high-performance controllers. Motorola's conclusion was that a Z80 assembly-language port to the 68000 requires three times the code space and two times the clock speed of the Z80 system, thus increasing the system's cost substantially.

This result is of particular interest if further development in the Mix Controller would require a more powerful processor. Motorola's assessment of an assembly-language port suggests[16] that the code-size and clock-speed penalties may be unacceptable, due to the far-reaching hardware changes that would be necessary to support the new processor. Other changes to the system would be required to make a processor switch attractive. The most obvious solution would be to use a high-level language (e.g. C) when switching to a new and faster processor, and optimize in assembly language wherever necessary. Since the Mix Controller is coded entirely in assembly language, the new C code would have to be written from scratch. Due to the compartmentalization of the bulk of the software in our scheme, this would not be inordinately difficult. Moreover, many of the routines written in the later stages of the project were pseudo-coded in high-level language prior to assembly-language coding! Ultimately the arguments against moving to a high-level language revolve

---

16 The analysis for ports to other processor families is likely to be similar, as their architectures have many of the same features.

almost exclusively around the potential inefficiencies (due to the increased number of instructions and procedure- or function-calling overheads) that are commonly associated with high-level languages when compared to well-written assembly language code.[17] We conclude, not surprisingly, that the move to a more powerful processor and / or programming in a high-level language would incur substantial one-time costs, particularly in capital outlay and initial debugging and testing. However, the actual re-coding of the state variables, filters and commands would be very straightforward, perhaps even automatic, and hence the costs directly associated with our DRCS structure would depend primarily on this rote chore.

Modular systems can often be upgraded with new hardware to improve performance or remain competitive. For example, the Nakamichi 1000 R-DAT digital audio tape recorder "features a modular design to accommodate future upgrades as A/D- and D/A-converter technology improves" [Har89, p. 114]. By using this hardware-independent scheme, only a small part of the DRCS code (analogous to a *driver*) needs to be rewritten in order to use the new hardware. In the DRCS described, support for a new DRCD will involve new input and output filters, and a new state variable. Upgrading DRCDs requires new filters only, assuming that the representation used for the state variable has sufficient resolution to take advantage of the new DRCD. Thus the costs associated with upgrading system components remain low due to the simplicity of the upgrade procedure and the fact that it can be performed independently of the rest of the system.

---

[17] There are some issues with the hardware, too, notably the little-endian byte ordering of the Z80 vs. the big-endian byte ordering of the 68k series.

5.11.6 Reliability of Implementation

Many programmers have resisted a formalized approach to assessing the reliability of their creations, as they feel that reliability theory is an arcane and needlessly complex subject.

> Unfortunately, many engineers and managers think of reliability and quality as numerical predictions developed by support functions, rather than design approaches. [Pri88, p. 11]

Often the methods they employ and the tools they use have matured over time into a position of pre-eminence partly due to their own reliability (and the resultant perceived quality of the code they help produce). For a programmer approaching a complex DRCS, an assessment of reliability will invariably evolve out of understandability, maintainability, basic design, and modularity of the code (these are issues beyond fundamental reliability concerns, issues and programming methodologies). It may be impossible to properly quantify the reliability of some real-time systems [But93].

The proposed approach has contributed greatly to the reliability of the system. Considerable accelerated (heavy-load) and regression testing was performed over the first few years that our DRCS software structure was employed. Very few failures were recorded, and they were all due to coding errors. These, in turn, were usually due to a failure to translate information correctly from the specification to the implementation. We attribute this low error rate to the simplicity of the input and output filters, with their clearly defined inputs (user activity, state variables) and outputs (state variables, DRCD control words), respectively. Only rarely did any other system information affect the activity of the filters. Fault detection and fault correction are easily accomplished whenever state variables are modified -- the two primary failure modes, out-of-bounds conditions (usually due to aberrations in the system's input domain) and conflicting state variables (see Appendix A), are easily resolved. Since the relationship between user input and DRCD activity was rarely obtuse, we found it easy to verify the proper operation of each DRCS function, either directly through the UI or perhaps through macros.

It is well-known [Mye76] that the probability of finding a software error is highest, and the cost of fixing the error is lowest, in the earliest stages of a design. Additionally, in the matter of software quality assurance -- often achieved through exhaustive regression testing -- the low number of errors found to-date suggests that the probability of additional errors is also low [Mye76]. The long-term operation and testing of a working system has demonstrated that the combination of our software structures is reliable. The basic soundness of our approach has been demonstrated in the extremely low levels of maintenance that have been required of the system's commands.

Since our software structure discourages interaction between DRCS functions, it was always easy to modify a particular DRCS function knowing that its new behavior ought to be completely independent of any other system activity. In those cases where this was found not to be true, it was always due to an out-of-bounds condition of another part of the system, which disappeared after correction. This orthogonality allowed us to completely revamp entire portions of the system without any effect on the rest of the DRCS functions. For example, we added the bit-control arguments for switch-type commands without any changes to other commands or to the command structure.

We also consider the effects of unreliable DRCDs on our system. The DRCS's input and output filters can be coded to reject any out-of-bounds values destined for or coming from the state variables, and to restore the corresponding state variable to an acceptable value. Since the DRCS's functions interact only via the state variables, and not through the actual devices, improperly functioning devices cannot damage the current state of the system. More sophisticated means of dealing with failures of certain types of devices [Mar90] can be implemented by rewriting the device filters.

5.11.7 Benefits of Implementation

The low costs of programming, testing and maintaining the system, as well as its demonstrated very high reliability, are two major benefits of our implementation using the proposed scheme for structuring DRCS software. A large part of the success of the proposed scheme can also be gauged by the performance of the system. Because the software and hardware of a DRCS are intertwined, its performance can only be analyzed by looking at the system as a whole. There are three major areas of interest -- normal operation, snapshot recall and automation.

The first goal was to be able to operate under any conceivable UI load with a frame rate of no worse than 1/30s. This involved hundreds of hours of actual user operation, as well as worst-case non-automated and automated operation with aggregate moves numbering in the tens of thousands, concentrated in small time periods. By "ticking" a 30fps clock once each time through the system's main arbiter's main loop, we were able to compare it with a real-time clock, and show that in fact under a light load the console is operating at a frame rate of about 1/120s. As more and more user activity is brought to bear, it degrades to near 1/30s.

Because of the parallel processing, user activity spread over several modules has much less of a detrimental effect on system performance than activity concentrated within a single module. By examining 30 seconds of real-time automation we were able to create an automation file via off-line editing that contained the maximum number of events that a single module could execute while maintaining 30fps synchronization with an external source. This automation data was replicated 11 times to create a large automation file for multiple I/O modules. This automation was then executed in a console with 2 to 11 modules fitted, and the results recorded. By having the console replay this automation with its internal clock free-running (i.e. as fast as possible, one tick per unsynchronized frame), we showed that the console's shared-memory interconnect scheme limited the maximum degradation of the frame rate to 10% when all of the system's modules were heavily loaded. The results are shown in Table 14.

Table 14: Real-Time Performance Degradation Due to Multiple Processors

# of Processors Active in Mix	Measured Time (hh:mm:ss:ff)
2	00:00:29:15
3	00:00:29:05
4	00:00:28:29
5	00:00:28:13
6	00:00:28:00
7	00:00:27:19
8	00:00:27:08
9	00:00:26:26
10	00:00:26:12
11	00:00:26:05

Snapshot recall required that the entire console be reconfigured from a new snapshot within 1/30s. The combined execution time for all the act[] and show[] routines nearly exceeded this specification. The solution was to preclude all function command execution in any frame that included a snapshot recall, as the effect of the commands would be annulled by the snapshot recall anyway. We also considered the option of storing snapshots in a "pre-computed" form, ready for immediate delivery to the Audio Mainframe and User Interface. However, discussions with users made it clear that continuous recall of snapshots in consecutive frames was wholly unnecessary. Hence this optimization was considered too costly in terms of programming effort, added complexity and memory consumed, and was not implemented.

Perhaps the greatest benefit of the proposed scheme is evident when automation comes into play. Once we were able to manage the automation database efficiently, automated operation became a reality. The console's performance under automation is actually better than under equivalent manual operation, as less processing is required of the User Input (little or no activity per frame, so for example pot and fader hysteresis algorithms are inactive), but the commands are still being executed. As a mix develops the layering of user input presents the system with a stream of commands beyond anything a user could do with ten fingers, so there is always an upper bounds on how many mix events the console can handle. The automation software ensured that there were no duplications of like commands in the event list for each frame, and was able to sustain real-time automated playback with up to 60-80% of all the controls actively changing.

5.11.8 Disadvantages of Implementation

Because of its size, in our implementation system reliability is a function of a combination of serial and parallel components. "Notice that the parallel system ... is more reliable than any of its individual components. This is a general characteristic of parallel components and their raison d'être" [Gra89, p. 114]. While not redundant, there is large-scale parallelism in the I/O functions of our implementation because of their standardized structure and their great number. Failures of the I/O function code would usually manifest themselves as a portion of the system's functionality no longer corresponding to the user's expectations. These were often very hard to detect, as they had no effect on the rest of the system. Hence some errors in the implementation could go undetected for a considerable period of time. A background task dedicated to verifying the correctness of the interface(s) with respect to the system's current state would be invaluable. Most failures were due to the activity of other, unrelated software processes impinging on the code and data memory of the function in question -- only improper coding practices and insufficient protection were to blame.

5.11.9 Summary

An analysis of our method and of an implementation of a large-scale system using this method indicates that it is worthy of consideration for the software design of digital remotely-controlled systems. Among its salient features are:

- Low Cost: From a programmer's perspective, it is easy to learn, to adapt to hardware requirements, and to fit into a larger software system. For a particular system, it is easy to implement, test, debug and maintain. It is an uncomplicated, hierarchical, complete approach to integrating I/O functions into a DRCS. The resulting high-performance code can be further optimized if necessary, but at a cost in flexibility.
- High Reliability: The simplicity, standardization, minimal connectedness and potential for error detection and correction all contribute towards a precise design that is resistant to typical programming and operating errors. If they do occur, errors can

be easily corrected without detrimental effect on other portions of the system.

- Other Benefits: It is general-purpose, applicable to any digital hardware, independent of programming language, amenable to automated tools, produces high-quality, high-performance code and assists in the creation of high-level system functionality. It has only minor drawbacks.

The results of the analysis are tabulated in Table 15.

Table 15: Benefits and Disadvantages of Method and Implementation

	Benefits	Disadvantages
Method	• simplicity of application • only basic knowledge of devices is required to implement methodology • does not require expert programming experience • programming-language independent • prescribed solutions to special cases • completely defines software for I/O chain • can safely handle entire UI domain • allows for code-size or execution-speed optimizations • code has extremely regular structure • low programming cost • precise design contributes to reliable code	• programmer appreciation dependent on an understanding of the software as whole • specifying representations remains difficult because of a lack of rules • in large systems, replication of filters becomes tedious

Table 15 (cont'd): Benefits and Disadvantages of Method and Implementation

	Benefits	Disadvantages
Implementation	• low cost coding, testing, inspecting, maintenance and support • high performance • replacement costs primarily dependent on choice(s) of new hardware and software, and not on DRCS structure • highly modular construction • deterministic execution of I/O chain • extremely reliable • faults usually trivial to correct • near-zero maintenance • local and global functional upgrades are easily implemented • no single-point, primary failure mode	• often difficult to perceive failures due to scale and parallelism of system • high effort and expertise is required to modify assembly-language code

5.12 Chapter Summary

Had we implemented each of the system's input-output chain in a locally optimal way, without regard for the system as a whole, it is likely that the DRCS would become a hodgepodge of solutions and methodologies. The cost of replacing or upgrading particular portions would have become completely unpredictable, especially if the workings of each DRCS function had not been kept independent of all the others. The previous examples have demonstrated that there are usually tradeoffs to be had when optimizing a particular, modular, low-level block of code. The overhead imposed by the DRCS structure is minimal, and its orderly approach allows these optimizations to be made without deleterious effects on the rest of the system. Ongoing development has shown that new features can easily be incorporated, and new programmers can easily be added to a DRCS staff as the system continues to evolve. The isolation from unwanted details that the structure provides is highly appreciated by those programming the DRCS. The balance of benefits of this standardized approach outweigh the minor optimizations that a non-standardized approach might yield.

This DRCS software structure was developed and applied to a family of audio mixing consoles [Loc94] over the course of more than four years. During that time it underwent many revisions and modifications, some involving substantial re-coding and downtime. Today, with over 100 of these consoles in daily use throughout the world, this work forms the basis for its run-time operation. It was coded entirely in Assembly language, and currently the code consists of four separate 64K modules with actual utilization ranging from 20KB to 50KB of code and data. Within the four types of hardware modules, two are similar in their basic kernel, but support totally different DRCDs. The third module, the main arbiter of the system, has a somewhat different kernel, but it still uses the same command structure and shares many common routines with the others. The fourth module, dedicated to high-speed communications, makes extensive use of the command structure (but not of state variables, as it has no user-perceived system functions) to facilitate the passing of information among the system's many channels.

We summarize the results of our implementation by noting that the DRCS software fulfilled all of our earlier objectives. In particular, it achieves the external characteristics we desired:

- correctness, which can be tested on a function-by-function basis;
- usability, since the underlying functionality is hidden from the User Interface;
- efficiency, as minimal system resources are required;
- reliability, as each function can be individually tested;
- integrity and robustness, in that User Interface activity cannot turn the state variables into an invalid state;
- adaptability, since the state variables can be chosen to be in the most readable format for external access; and
- accuracy, due to the simple program flow from input to output through the filters by way of the state variables.

The DRCS software also achieves the internal characteristics we desired:

- maintainability, readability and testability, all due to the software's modular construction and regular structure;
- flexibility, as it can accommodate any DRCD;
- portability, made possible by its simplicity and minimal connectedness;
- reusability, as the method itself is applicable to DRCSs large and small and is hardware-independent; and
- understandability, as its having only a few basic concepts (state variables, input and output filters, snapshots, commands) makes it easily comprehensible.

Finally, in our particular implementation:

- Our structured software programming methodology has been quickly picked up by non-expert programmers and the resulting code quality has been very high;
- The resulting DRCS is easily extended, interfaced to, analyzed, monitored and constructed;

- The addition of new modules is facilitated by an easy-to-follow methodology -- sometimes tedious because of the scope of the module, but never difficult;

- Maintenance of the DRCS has been low and inexpensive. Once implemented, large portions of code have remained untouched for years while overall functionality has increased -- a high level of modularity was achieved;

- The modularity and minimal connectedness of the software structure has isolated each part of the system from changes and / or errors occurring elsewhere;

- Hardware changes due to upgrades are easily made in number and type without fundamental changes to the underlying software structure;

- Replacement costs are dictated by issues beyond ones directly associated with the proposed software structure;

- Standardized representations with state variables have accomplished real-time operation of console, minimum-size snapshot recall, and ease of development & debugging;

- Channel data is stored in 30-50% more bytes than are required by the physical layer;

- The system has the capability of recalling a snapshot in just under 1/30s;

- When running non-automated, the system has considerable leftover processing power -- this indicates that the underlying supporting structure consumes the "idle" power, and actual command execution is quite efficient;

- No repetition or duplication of conversion/format routines is required, now or in the future;

- Deterministic (i.e. will execute up to 60 commands per frame per channel, on average) command execution independent of source and destination channels;

- The software structure fits seamlessly into either a user-input or DRCS-action-oriented automation system. A choice of one over the other does not invalidate the other;

- The software structure achieved symbiosis with the underlying multiprocessor design. The overwhelming importance of the state variable, combined with the flexibility of a standardized and variable-length command set never prevented any new features from reaching realization; and

- Although automation is driven primarily by an external computer, the standardization of all command-based behavior eases the implementation of any advanced functionality one may want to inject into the console.

5.13 Future Developments and Research

Currently others are developing advanced automation capabilities for the system described above, and most of this work is done within the support computer, with simple hooks to the console's user interface. There are currently no plans (nor any perceived need) to substantially alter the DRCS scheme in further expansions of this system. However, it is almost certain that assembly language will be abandoned in the future in favor of coding in a higher-level language.

The analysis of, and many of the measures in this work are primarily qualitative, not quantitative. While quantitative results were obtained in several instances where competing methodologies were evaluated for inclusion in the basic software structure, the scope of quantitative analysis remained local to these small-scale evaluations. Low-level quantitative assessments of code size and execution speed were also used in many areas that were seen as critical to the overall performance of the system.[18] Finally, real-time performance evaluations of the system yielded measurable data.

---

[18] For example, the performance of the EuBus connection was improved some 30% through careful coding and concomitatnt changes to the hardware design with regard to multi-host bus arbitration.

It must be noted that all of these quantitative measures reflect the particular implementation, and are only indirectly related to the software methodology presented. In fact, some of the measures are more likely an indication of programmer prowess and the capabilities of the particular hardware/software combination than of our methodology. However, as software programming becomes more of an engineering discipline rather than a black art, we expect tools to become available that would allow for an objective and quantitative appraisal of the efficiencies we present in our scheme, and how it compares with other software structures. Our qualitative approach to DRCS software, resulting in a modular and simple structure, will lend itself well to both small-scale and large-scale future quantitative analysis. Areas that ought to be addressed via quantitative analysis include:

- optimal coding for code size and execution speed;
- a quantitative assessment of costs incurred when replacing digital components in an I/O chain;
- a measurement of system reliability taking into effect the parallel (and possibly redundant) combination of multiple, short serial I/O processes;
- the effect on performance when coding in a high-level language, and where assembly-language optimizations would still be required;
- the issue of "division of tasks," i.e. the effect(s) on code structure due to the number of processors employed; and
- a further investigation on the optimal structure for automated, real-time operation in a larger system.

Lastly, for the purposes of comparison with other software structures for DRCSs, it is instructive to review those measures of performance that would form the basis for a comparative analysis. These would include:

- a cost/benefit analysis of the programming effort and the resulting DRCS using our scheme;
- a realistic appraisal of the resistance to obsolescence of our scheme;
- an assessment of memory and clock cycles used to perform a particular I/O function;
- a study of processors, memory architectures and programming languages to reveal which ones are best suited to our scheme; and
- a look at the long-term costs (e.g. design, programming, testing, and warranty) incurred by an organization when applying our software structure to the creation of DRCSs.

Insofar as we have been able to obtain measures of performance for our implementation, we feel that it represents, for a reasonably low cost, a very high level of performance and reliability with only modest programming and subsequent maintenance efforts. We are confident that the proposed software methodology and the resulting DRCS software structure will compare favorably to other schemes in such an analysis.

CHAPTER 6
SUMMARY AND CONCLUSIONS

We have proposed a new methodology for programming digital remotely controlled systems to control digital remotely controllable devices. By analyzing the interplay between the user's perception of the system and the behavior of the I/O devices, we are able to translate a portion of the system specifications directly to a set of software specifications which, when coded via the guidelines of our methodology, implement the system's I/O functionality. This step-by-step procedure greatly simplifies the software design of such systems and guarantees a high level of performance and reliability at low cost.

Our approach is highly structured, involving only a few software constructs to handle all activity between the inputs and outputs. Its primary focus is on the user's perception of what the DRCS does. Once this perception is characterized, the software to support the DRCDs can be readily created and subsequently integrated into the rest of the design. We have shown that the combination of input and output filters, state variables and a command structure is all that is required to create a functional DRCS. Furthermore, these elements can easily be arranged to provide many higher-level system features such as recallability and automation. Our software structure is applicable to DRCSs of any size and is extensible to many different hardware architectures.

Our software structure is a powerful tool for creating a DRCS. As a paradigm for coding such systems, it demonstrates the power of separating the multiple layers of activity in the DRCS in a way that is both efficient and also enhances system reliability. Since each element of our scheme is individually comprehensible and can be independently coded, programmers need not retreat from the potentially overwhelming task of coding a DRCS from scratch. A real-world application of our scheme exposed some deficiencies due to issues we had not previously considered. However, these were easily solved without changing the underlying tenets of our software structure.

Our implementation also showed that even very large DRCSs can be created at low cost via our scheme. A system utilizing our software structure has proven to be robust, reliable, and ultimately quite powerful. We believe this is largely due to the "division of labor" in the software -- any part of the system is quickly and easily understood, as each subpart thereof is small in scope and size, and can be proven to work correctly with little effort. Largely because of this, our work is an excellent foundation for DRCS designs that are considerably more sophisticated than ones we originally envisioned.

In all facets of the design the old maxim "Simplify, Simplify, Simplify" was never forgotten. Great pride was taken in creating a system that is easy to understand, to debug, to introduce to new programmers, and most importantly, to work with as new features and performance are requested. The simplicity of our DRCS software enhances the system's reliability. At all times, however, we did not lose sight of the fact the elegance of the code and architecture were irrelevant if the system did not perform to specification.

There remain a few issues that have not been sufficiently deeply explored, but most of them are trivial. They are an issue only because we chose to write in assembly language, and hence many optimizations were much more obvious to us than had we written in a high-level language. A new approach to designing and creating embedded systems, called *co-synthesis* [Gup93], results in a concurrency of design for both hardware and software. The simplicity of the

DRCS software structure, and the regularity it imparts to the software written with it, suggest that it might adapt well to incorporation into automatic design tools such as this one. We are currently interested in evaluating how well our scheme performs in a more widely dispersed system, where external communications play a greater role.

REFERENCES

[Abr94]   MICHAEL ABRASH. *The Zen of Code Optimization*, The Coriolis Group, Scottsdale, Arizona, 1994.

[Abu86]   W. ABU-SUFAH, H.E. HUSMANN and D.J. KUCK. "On Input/Output Speedup in Tightly Coupled Multiprocessors," *IEEE Transactions on Computers C-35*, 6 (1986), 520-529.

[Bec93]   ANDREW P. BECK. "Developing 80x86-Based Embedded Systems," *The C Users Journal 11*, 3 (1993), 45-52.

[Bro75]   FREDERICK P. BROOKS JR. *The Mythical Man-Month*, Addison-Wesley, Menlo Park, California, 1975.

[Bur94]   BRAD BURGESS, NASR ULLAH, PETER VAN OVEREN, and DEENE OGDEN. "The PowerPC 603 Microprocessor," *Communications of the ACM 37*, 6 (1994), 34 - 41.

[But93]   RICKY W. BUTLER and GEORGE B. FINELLI. "The Infeasability of Quantifying the Reliability of Life-Critical Real-Time Software," *IEEE Transactions on Software Engineering 19*, 1 (1993), 3-12.

[Buy94]   "Buyer's Guide," *Embedded Systems Programming Product News*, Miller Freeman, Inc., San Francisco, Summer 1994.

[Cat93]   DARREN CATHEY. "All Things Considered ... Important Factors in Choosing a Real-Time Development System," *Real-Time Magazine 6*, 2 (1993), 87-96.

[Cor94]   JOHN P. CORTEZ. "Moving into the Mainstream – A8," *Autoweek 44*, 20 (1994), 22-24.

[Cri93]   CRISP G.R.A.S.P. "A Guide to the 5ESS," *2600 10*, 2 (1993), 4-11.

[DeF87]   STEVE DE FURIA and JOE SCACCIAFERRO. *The MIDI Resource Book*, Third Earth Publishing, Inc., Pompton Lakes, New Jersey, 1987.

[Fad92]   FAISDAL FADUL and FRANSISCO BAS. "Stand-Alone Programmable Controller for Time-Critical Robotic Systems," *Robotics & Computer-Integrated Manufacturing 9*, 3 (1992), 191-199.

[Gra89]   DORIS LLOYD GRASH. *A Primer of Reliability Theory*, John Wiley & Sons, New York, 1989.

[Gup93]   RAJESH KUMAR GUPTA. "Co-Synthesis of Hardware and Software for Digital Embedded Systems," *Doctoral Dissertation*, Stanford University, 1993.

[Har87]   DAVID HAREL. *Algorithmics : The Spirit of Computing*, Addison-Wesley Publishing Co., Menlo Park, California, 1987.

[Har89]   ROBERT HARLEY. "Nakamichi 1000 R-DAT Recorder," *Stereophile 12*, 11, (1989), 112-122.

[Hol88]   TOMLINSON HOLMAN. "Postproduction Systems and Editing," *Audio Engineering Handbook*, K. Blair Benson Ed., McGraw-Hill, Inc., New York, 1988, 14.28-14.44.

[Hor89]   PAUL HOROWITZ and WINFIELD HILL. *The Art of Electronics (Second Edition)*, Cambridge University Press, Cambridge, 1989.

[Hor90]   MARK R. HORTON. *Portable C Software*, Prentice Hall, Englewood Cliffs, New Jersey, 1990.

[Hub87]   DAVID MILES HUBER. "The Edit Screen," *Audio Production Techniques for Video*, Howard W. Sams & Co., Indianapolis, Indiana, 1987.

[Inv93]   "An Investigation of the THERAC 60 Accident", *IEEE Computer*, July 1993.

[Kal93]   ANDREW E. KALMAN. "Command Language for Digital Communication," *pending U.S. Patent application*, 1993.

[Kir91]   N. KIRCANSKI, M. VUKOBRATOVIC, B. KARAN, M. KIRCANSKI and A. TIMCENKO. "Multiprocessor Control System for Industrial Robots," *Robotics & Computer-Integrated Manufacturing 8*, 2 (1991), 77-86.

[Led87]   HENRY LEDGRAD. *Professional Software, Vol. II, Programming Practice*, Addison Wesley, Reading, Massachusetts, 1987.

[Loc94]   DAVE LOCKWOOD. "Euphonix CS2000," *Audio Media 42* (1994), 44-50.

[Mar90]   KEITH MARZULLO. "Tolerating Failures of Continuous-Valued Sensors," *ACM Transactions on Computer Systems 8*, 4 (1990), 284-304.

[McC88]   CARMA MCCLURE. "The CASE for Structured Development," *PC Tech Journal 6*, 8 (1988), 51-67.

[McC93]   STEVE MCCONNELL. *Code Complete: A Practical Handbook of Software Construction*, Microsoft Press, Redmond, Washington, 1993.

[Mey93]   SCOTT MEYER, ROGER OBERG and DOUG WALTON. *XVT Technical Overview*, XVT Software Inc., Boulder, Colorado, 1993.

[Mil93]   JOHN P. MILLWARD. "Electronic Systems Architecture," *Automotive Engineering 101*, 4 (1993), 15-17.

[Mot82]   MOTOROLA MC68000 APPLICATIONS GROUP, MOTOROLA SEMICONDUCTOR PRODUCTS - AUSTIN, *CNVZ80 - Z80 SOURCE TO MC68000 SOURCE UTILITY*, from Motorola Freeware BBS, 1982.

[Mot90]   MOTOROLA, INC. *MC68332 User's Manual*, Author, Phoenix, Arizona, 1990.

[Mus85]   *Musical Instrument Digital Interface 1.0 Detailed Specification*, International MIDI Association, Hollywood, California, 1985.

[Mye76]   GLENFORD J. MYERS. *Software Reliability – Principles and Practices*, John Wiley & Sons, New York, 1976.

[Nat90]   NATIONAL SEMICONDUCTOR, INC. *Data Communications/LAN/ UARTs Handbook*, Author, Santa Clara, California, 1990.

[Neu91]   NEURON DATA INC. *Neuron Data Open Interface Technical Overview*, Author, Palo Alto, California, 1991.

[Nip80]   NIPPON KOGAKU K.K. *Nikon F3 Repair Manual*, Author, Tokyo, Japan, 1980.

[Nor92]   THOMAS J. NORTON. "Industry Update:US," *Stereophile 15*, 10 (1992), 47-51.

[Nor94]   THOMAS J. NORTON. "Industry Update: Germany", *Stereophile 17*, 4 (1994), 37-39.

[Oeh93]   WILLIAM OEHME and STEVEN BROSKY. "High Times for Realtime Computers," *Machine Design 66*, 5 (1993), 44-50.

[Pat90]   DAVID A. PATTERSON and JOHN L. HENNESSEY. *Computer Architecture: A Quantitative Approach*, Morgan Kauffman Publishers, Inc., San Mateo, California, 1990.

[Pet93]   JOHN M. PETERS. "Automation Control with Improved Operator/System Interface," *U. S. Patent 5,243,513*, September 7, 1993.

[Pri88]   JOHN W. PRIEST. *Engineering Design for Producability and Reliability*, Marcel Dekker, Inc., New York, New York and Basel, Switzerland, 1988.

[Que88]   DANIEL QUEEN. "Standards and Recommended Practices," *Audio Engineering Handbook*, K. Blair Benson, Ed., McGraw-Hill, Inc, New York, New York, 1988.

[Sch93]   KLAUS SCHNITZER, "850CSi," *Roundel : The Magazine of the BMW Car Club of America 24*, 10 (1993), 24-26.

[Shi94]   JULIE SHIPNES and MIKE PHILLIP. "A Modular Approach to Motorola PowerPC Compilers," *Communications of the ACM 37*, 6 (1994), 56-63.

[Sho92]   R. SHOURESTIC. "A Course in μP-Based Control Systems," *IEEE Control Systems*, June 1992.

[Spa94]   PIERRE SPARACO, "Autopilot a Factor in A330 Accident," *Aviation Week and Space Technology 141*, 2 (1994), 26-27.

[Sta89]   JOHN A. STANKOVIC. "Decentralized Decision Making for Task Reallocation in a Hard Real-Time System," *IEEE Transactions on Computers 38*, 3 (1989), 341-355.

[Sta93]   MICHAEL PAUL STAVROU. "A New Approach to Assignable Control-Surface Design," *Journal of the Audio Engineering Society 41*, 7/8 (1993), 556-563.

[Tan91]   WEI SIONG TAN, SAMUEL H. RUSS and CECIL O. ALFORD. "GT-EP: A Novel High-Performance Real-Time Architecture," *ACM SIGARCH Computer Architectural News 19*, 3 (1991), 12-21.

[Tay86]   D.J. TAYLOR and C.-J. H. SEGER. "Robust Storage Structures for Crash Recovery," *IEEE Transactions on Computers C-35*, 4 (1986), 288-295.

[Tea94]   B.F. TEASLEY. "The Effects of Naming Style and Expertise on Program Comprehension." *International Journal of Human Computer Studies 40*, 5 (1994), 757-770.

[Tho93]   TOM THOMPSON. "PowerPC Performs for Less," *BYTE 18*, 9 (1993), 56-74.

[Tör92]   MARTIN TÖRNGREN and JAN WIKANDER. "Real-Time Control of Physically Distributed Systems," *Computers Electrical Engineering 18*, 1 (1992), 51-72.

[Tra90]   MARTIN TRACY. "ZEN for Embedded Systems," *Dr. Dobb's Journal 15*, 1 (1990), 38-46.

[Tur50]   ALAN M. TURING. "Computing Machinery and Intelligence," *Mind 59*, 236, (1950), 433-460.

[War90]   MICHAEL WARD. *Software That Works*, Academic Press, Inc., San Diego, California, 1990.

[Win80]   DAVID WINKEL and FRANKLIN PROSSER. *The Art of Digital Design*, Prentice-Hall, Englewood Cliffs, New Jersey, 1980.

[Win93]   WIND RIVER SYSTEMS, INC. *VxWorks Promotional Brochure*, Author, Alameda, California, 1993.

[Wir76]   NIKLAUS WIRTH. *Algorithms + Data Structures = Programs*, Prentice-Hall, Englewood Cliffs, New Jersey, 1976.

[Zil77]   ZILOG, INC. *Z80-CPU/Z80A-CPU Technical Manual*, Author, Cupertino, California, 1977.

APPENDIX A
RESOLVING SPECIAL CASES

A.1 Conflicting State Variables

In a DRCS a conflict can arise where, due to the organization of the user interface and/or the arrangement of the DRCDs in the system, the setting of one state variable is at odds with another. A good example is one where the configuring of one user setting (say a switch) leads to an undesirable audio feedback path in another part of the system. The DRCS designer must identify "safe" values for interdependent state variables so that these "illegal" system configurations are prevented.

Due to the nature of the DRCS, the scope of a command for a particular user input will generally not involve the state variable of the conflicting DRCD elsewhere. So this becomes a question of where to put the code that resolves the conflict.

There are two different cases of conflicting state variables -- 1) where a conflict exists within a particular state variable (e.g. where the state variable is a collection of bits controlling, say, a number of independent switches) and 2), where one state variable conflicts with another.

A.2 State Variables With Illegal States

In the first case, keeping in mind that set[], act[] and show[] are the only functions tied directly to the conflicting state variable, the question becomes where to put a piece of conflict-resolving code within the state variable's command. The two candidates are set[] and act[], as the conflict must be resolved before the control word reaches the DRCD.

The problem with putting the resolver in set[] is that the system breaks down if a snapshot with conflicting state variables is recalled. This can occur due to an error in the snapshot, due to cumulative command playback with act[] and show[] disabled or it can occur due to the selective recall of only a portion of a snapshot -- a very useful feature, as it in effect provides the user with the ability to recall settings that affect just a user-specified portion of the DRCS.

By putting the resolver in act[] we can guarantee that the DRCD will never receive an incorrect control word regardless of how the state variables are manipulated on the input side of the system. This approach can be extended to provide efficient error detection and correction of state variables system-wide, since it is performed only when a new control word is destined for the DRCD in question.

In cases where an immediately apparent conflict or value is known (e.g. out-of-bounds error), the state variable's set[] command can simply prevent the illegal entry from being accepted by the DRCS .

A.3 Sets of Conflicting State Variables

The second case is one where a set of state variables can hold values that conflict with one another. The approach in the case above is less applicable here because sets of conflicting state variables require that multiple commands be executed in order to guarantee the integrity of the DRCDs. Hence this type of conflict requires an approach where the conflict is resolved in the set[] stage of the current command.

Such an approach is elegant and well-integrated as it confines changes to the state variable to the set[] stage, where we expect it. Since this resolver action may result in a change to a state variable outside this command, we must ensure that this outside state variable's act[] and show[] are also called. As an example, if state variables x and y have the potential to conflict, their commands should look like:

```
x:    set[x, new_val]          y:    set[y, new_val]
      act[x]                          act[y]
      act[y]                          act[x]
      show[x]                         show[y]
      show[y]                         show[x]
```

where set[x] and set[y] are functions of both x and y and may change both x and y if a conflict is found.

This approach does have the drawback of being unable to handle state variable conflict that arise due to system operation where state variables are not written by set[], e.g. snapshot recall. In these cases either the approach mentioned above for illegal state variables or a standalone snapshot-conflict resolver is required.

APPENDIX B
STATE VARIABLE REPRESENTATIONS

B.1 Alternate Representations

The flexibility afforded a DRCS by its software structure means that there is always the opportunity to tailor its software structure to optimally perform in the given application. This appendix discusses some of these alternate structures and where they are most applicable. Note that oftentimes, if system resources allow, a DRCS can be created with more than one structures as long as they do not conflict with one another (easier said than done!).

B.2 DRCD Format Representation

The DRCD format alternate representation uses the DRCD control word as its central unit of information in order to describe the DRCS's current state. Since each control word is tied directly to the physical implementation in each DRCD, and has a unique link to the user input, it rapidly becomes unwieldy and unmanageable in larger systems. Its main advantage is that since the DRCD control word is always known, little or no processing is required by the system in order to update the DRCDs due to snapshot recall. This is in contrast to a DRCS employing the state variable approach where the state variable's format is not the same as the format of the DRCD control word.

External queries are greatly complicated by such a representation, as the external process must know the details of the physical implementation of the DRCD in order to make sense of the data queried from the system. Changes to the DRCDs therefore require changes to any externally interfacing process, greatly complicating the system upgrade picture.

In a system employing the DRCD format representation it is reasonable to expect the system architect do away with the second step of the three part input-to-output chain for the sake of simplicity. The reader will notice that for all intents and purposes this is what is happening in those cases of the state variable DRCS where the format of the state variable exactly matches the DRCD control word. In such systems the third step of the input-to-output chain is just a direct mapping of the state variable onto the DRCD.

B.3 User Input Representation

Moving to the other end of the system, one could choose to hold in memory only the state of the user input. The biggest disadvantage of this approach lies again in the fact that such a representation unnecessarily ties the system to the physical characteristics of the input devices.

APPENDIX C
LARGE SYSTEM DESIGN ISSUES

In any large software project the tasks of creation and maintenance are greatly simplified if the code is modular, consistent and conforming to some predetermined standard. In a large DRCS, with its strong ties to actual physical hardware, the plethora of issues that must be addressed by the software can rapidly overwhelm the designer. This appendix touches on a few points designed to make the system more reliable and easier to work with.

<u>Use a minimum number of representations</u>. As an example, imagine a large, multiple-input, multiple-output system charged with controlling signal levels. Furthermore, imagine that the level-controlling DRCD's consist of 8-, 12- and 16-bit DACs from various manufacturers in a variety of different circuit configurations. By picking a single state variable format to represent level (in dB, for example) the system will require only one group of functions to manipulate levels in the DRCS. As long as each representation has sufficient range and resolution to handle all current and foreseeable DRCD demands then adding new parts to the system should be very easy.

<u>Use consistent representations</u>. As an example, a DRCS may have a large number of digitally-controlled switches, each one using either 1=ON or 1=OFF control voltage polarity. The recommended state variable for such devices is simply one or more bitfields with each bit representing a binary control voltage. By having the foresight to decide on one particular representation (e.g. 0=ON, 1=OFF, so-called "active low") for the entire system one can maintain consistency

throughout all routines that deal with controlling and displaying the status of these devices. For those devices whose polarity is opposite to the chosen representation, all that is required is a simple bit-complement operation on the state variable in act[] just prior to sending the control word to the DRCD.

Avoid arbitrary hardware design decisions. Even though the most twisted hardware architecture can be hidden and isolated from view within the system by software, this situation is only detrimental to the performance of the system. As an example, if a user is to select the ON/OFF state of eight grouped switches numbered 1 through 8, it behooves the software designer to make the hardware designer aware of this so that he creates a byte-long DRCD control word with the bits arranged in the same pattern. Sometimes this may prove impossible due to cost or space constraints placed on the hardware. Again, the solution is to put a translator in act[] to map the ordered bits in the state variable to the not-so-ordered bits in the DRCD control byte.

Choose meaningful names. Particularly when introducing the system's code to uninitiated programmers, careful choices of labels, functions and variables can greatly ease the learning experience. In programs written in high-level languages, naming is important for the comprehension by novices, but much less so by experienced programmers [Tea94]. Consistency is also very important.

Carry incremental improvements only so far. In many designs, no matter how carefully planned out at the start, there will come a time when obvious improvements to the system can and should be made. The danger lies in doing too many incremental improvements instead of a single, all-out version update to support the changes. Programmer productivity falls dramatically with the "rip-up and retry" approach.

APPENDIX D
CODE COMPUTATIONS

D.1 Computation of Call/Return Overhead for Commands

Below is an expanded listing of the Z80 assembly-language code to implement the OUT1 command. Macros have been converted to in-line instructions, and subroutines have been fully expanded. Given the hardware constraints of the system, it is considered to be well-optimized for speed without requiring an excess of hard-coded code to interface to the relay and LED hardware. The overhead of maintaining individual set[], act[] and show[] routines that are combined to form commands is shown in bold print. The extra instructions add less than 0.5% to the code size and an equal percentage to the code execution time. Several code blocks would require fewer instructions with a processor having a more versatile set of registers or one with a longer wordlength. Z80 instruction set figures are from Zilog [Zil77].

Table 16: Call/Return Overhead Summary

Instruction	# bytes	# clock cycles
call set_OUT_1_src	**3**	**17**
and 00111111b	1	4
ld IY,(base2_ChSnapshot)	4	20
ld (IY+OUT_1_src-128),A	3	19
ret	**1**	**10**
call act_OUT_1_src	**3**	**17**
call rd_AM_block_ptr	3	17
ld DE,AM_block_ptr	3	10
ld HL,(base_Chmem)	3	16
add HL,DE	1	11
ld E,(HL)	1	7

- 148 -

```
        inc HL                                          1        6
        ld D,(HL)                                       1        7
        push DE                                         1       11
        pop IX                                          2       14
        ret                                             1       10
ld (IX+AM_STEERING_BYTE),AM_STEER_SRC_1_2               4       19
ld IY,(base2_ChSnapshot)                               4       20
ld A,(IY+OUT_1_src-128)                                3       19
cpl                                                    1        4
ld (IX+AM_DATA_BYTE1),A                                3       19
ld IY,(base2_ChSnapshot)                               4       20
ld A,(IY+OUT_2_src-128)                                3       19
cpl                                                    1        4
ld (IX+AM_DATA_BYTE_2),A                               3       19
call save_new_AM_block                                 3       17
        push IX                                         2       15
        pop BC                                          1       10
        inc BC                                          1        6
        inc BC                                          1        6
        inc BC                                          1        6
        inc BC                                          1        6
        ld DE,AM_block_ptr                              3       10
        ld HL,(base_Chmem)                              3       16
        add HL,DE                                       1       11
        ld (HL),C                                       1        7
        inc HL                                          1        6
        ld (HL),B                                       1        7
        ld DE,AM_block_count                            3       10
        ld HL,(base_Chmem)                              3       16
        add HL,DE                                       1       11
        inc (HL)                                        1       11
        ret                                             1       10
    ret                                                 1       10
jp show_OUT_1_src                                       3       17
    ld DE,mp_LEDs_ptr                                   3       10
    call rd_Channel_word                                3       17
        ld HL,(base_Chmem)                              3       16
        add HL,DE                                       1       11
        ld E,(HL)                                       1        7
        inc HL                                          1        6
        ld D,(HL)                                       1        7
        ret                                             1       10
    ld (mp_LEDs_ptr),DE                                 4       20
    ld DE,OUT1_mp_LEDs                                  3       10
    ld HL,(base_Chdat)                                  3       16
    add HL,DE                                           3       11
    ld (mp_LED_ctrl_tbl_ptr),HL                         1       16
    ld IY,(base2_ChSnapshot)                            3       20
    ld A,(IY+OUT_1_src-128)                             4       19
    cpl                                                 3        4
    ld C,A                                              1        4
    call show_OUT                                       1       17
        ld E,M1_source                                  3        7
        call prep_mp_OUT_LEDs                           2       17
            ld HL,(mp_LED_ctrl_tbl_ptr)                 3       16
            ld E,(HL)                                   3        7
            inc HL                                      1        6
            ld B,(HL)                                   1        7
```

inc HL	1	6
ld (mp_LED_ctrl_tbl_ptr),HL	1	16
ld HL,(mp_LED_SR_ptr)	3	16
ld D,0	3	7
add HL,DE	2	11
ret	1	10
bit M1_source,C	1	8
call show_OUT_bit	2	17
ld A,(HL)	3	7
jr Z,$	1	7/12
ld D,A	2	4
ld A,B	1	4
cpl	1	4
or D	1	4
ld (HL),A	1	7
ret	1	10
$:and B	1	4
ld (HL),A	1	7
ret	1	10
(repeated 5 more times for M2...L4)	195	1095/1120
ret	1	10
total:	366	2092/2117

D.2 Computation of Switch-Type Command Preprocessor Overhead

Below is a Z80 expansion listing of the switch-type command preprocessor (an assembly-language macro) used to facilitate the control of individual bits through a single command execution. This particular routine is suitable to all 8-bit switch-type commands, and allows for the clearing, setting and writing of all bits simultaneously, as well as the turning ON and OFF and toggling of individual bits. The routine uses table lookup to execute one of six subroutines corresponding to the CLR/OFF/ON/SET/TGL/WR subcommand. Prefacing a typical command's set[], act[], show[] sequence with this processor increases the code size and execution times by approximately 5%.

Table 17: Command Preprocessor Overhead Summary

Instruction	# bytes	# clock cycles
_rtn_Prop_Mod_svar_arg state_variable		
ld DE,state_variable	3	10
call rtn_Property_Modify_arg_via_svar	3	17
ld A,(mc_arg)	3	13

```
          cp WR_CMD+1                           2        7
          jr NC, bad_Prop_Mod_subcmd           2        7/12
          call get_Sapshot_ptr                 3        17
            ld HL,(base_ChSnapshot)            3        16
            add HL,DE                          1        11
            ret                                3        10
          ld B,(HL)                            1        7
          ld HL,Property_Modify_subcmds        3        10
          call call_via_table                  3        17
            ld D,0                             2        7
            ld E,A                             1        4
            add HL,DE                          1        11
            add HL,DE                          1        11
            ld E,(HL)                          1        7
            inc HL                             1        6
            ld D,(HL)                          1        7
            ex DE,HL                           1        4
            jp (HL)                            1        4
          ld B,A                               1        4
          xor A                                1        4
          ld A,B                               1        4
          ret                                  1        10
bad_Prop_Mod_subcmd:
          ld A,1                               1        7
          or A                                 1        4
          ret                                  1        10

Prop_Mod_subcmd_CLR:
          xor A                                1        4
          ret                                  1        10

Prop_Mod_subcmd_OFF:
          ld A,(mc_arghi)                      3        13
          cpl                                  1        4
          and B                                1        4
          ret                                  1        10

Prop_Mod_subcmd_ON:
          ld A,(mc_arghi)                      3        13
          or B                                 1        4
          ret                                  1        10

Prop_Mod_subcmd_SET:
          ld A,11111111b                       2        7
          ret                                  1        10

Prop_Mod_subcmd_TGL:
          ld A,(mc_arghi)                      3        13
          xor B                                1        4
          ret                                  1        10

Prop_Mod_subcmd_WR:
          ld A,(mc_arghi)                      3        13
          ret                                  1        10
```

	worst-case total:	49	256

APPENDIX E
EXAMPLES OF DRCS HARDWARE

The following four pages contain schematic diagrams for selected parts of the implementation. All four schematics contain hardware for more than one DRCS function. Figure 24 shows meter-panel LEDs for all four channels of an I/O module.

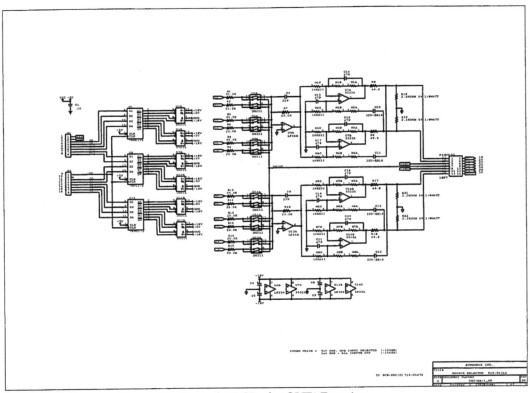

Figure 23: Control DRCDs for OUT1 Function

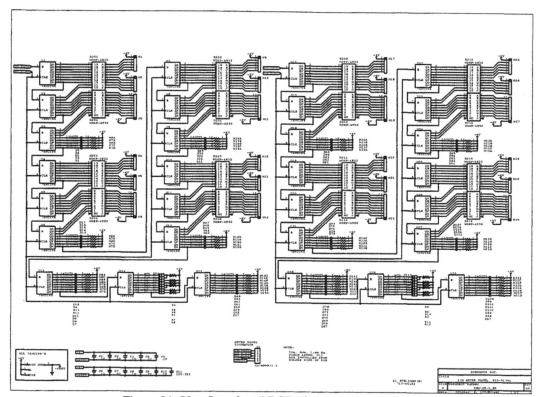

Figure 24: User Interface DRCDs for OUT1 Function

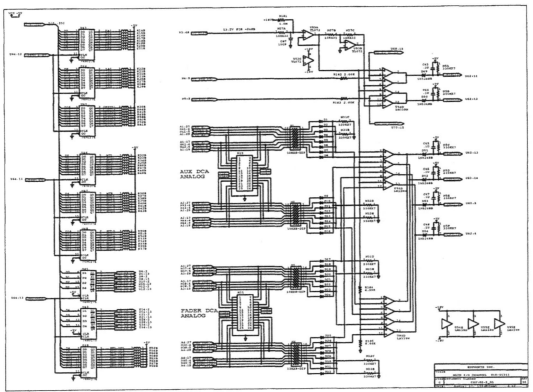

Figure 25: Control DRCDs for Upper Fader Multitrack Assign Function

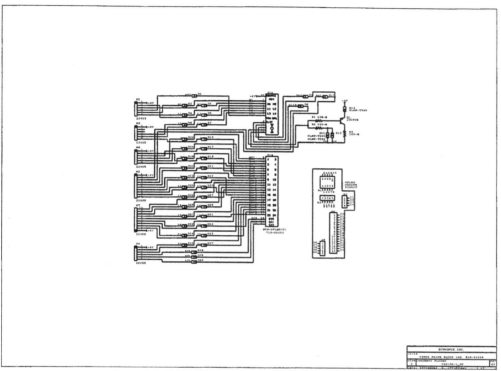

Figure 26: Upper Fader Multitrack Assign LED Board

APPENDIX F
DISSERTATION CREATION NOTES

This work was researched, tested and evaluated -- and this dissertation was written -- over the course of much time on several computers.

All programming, testing and debugging was done on a collection of '286, '386 and '486 computers with assemblers and compilers from Microtec Research, Inc. and with code management tools from a variety of suppliers. IBM's PE2 was used as a code editor running under DOS. DOS computers were linked via LANtastic networking software.

This dissertation was composed on an Apple Macintosh Quadra 700 with 8MB RAM, a 240MB hard disk and a SONY 17" CPD-1604S color monitor. Software included Microsoft Word 5.1a for composition, Claris MacDraw II 1.1 for most drawings, Delta Tao Software Color MacCheese 1.03 Cocker Spaniel for pixel-based drawings, and Apple ResEdit 2.1.1 for grabbing and creating icons. It is set primarily in 12-point Palatino, with 10-point italic Courier used for code fragments. Schematic diagrams were generated from OrCAD in EPS form, and then taken to a Mac IIfx where they were translated via TechPool Software's Transverter Pro 1.5.1 into Adobe EPS format, after which they were scaled in Adobe Illustrator 5.0 to 36% where the figure legends were added. Where the Internet was used, a Global Village Teleport Gold 14,400bps modem was used with ZTerm 0.9gv for terminal use and QualComm Eudora 1.0b3 handled e-mail. All printing was done on an Hewlett-Packard LaserJet 4M laser printer at 600dpi connected to an AppleTalk network via Farallon's EtherWave EtherTalk Adapters.

The photographic illustrations in Chapter 5 are used with permission from Euphonix, Inc. and are courtesy Andy Wild. Some code fragments, as well as the schematics in Appendix D, are copyright Euphonix, Inc. and are used with permission.

All brand names and product names herein are trademarks, registered trademarks or trade names of their respective holders.

BIOGRAPHICAL SKETCH

Andrew Evangelos Kalman has a Bachelor of Science degree in electrical engineering from Stanford University and a Master of Science degree in electrical engineering from the University of Florida.

After working briefly at IBM's T.J. Watson Research Center and at Stanford Research Systems, Inc., Andrew co-founded Euphonix, Inc. in Palo Alto, California, with two associates and led the R&D team for several years. He is now Euphonix's Director of Special Projects.

I certify that I have read this study and that in my opinion it conforms to acceptable standards of scholarly representation and is fully adequate, in scope and quality, as a dissertation for the degree of Doctor of Philosophy.

John Staudhammer, Chair
Professor of Electrical Engineering

I certify that I have read this study and that in my opinion it conforms to acceptable standards of scholarly representation and is fully adequate, in scope and quality, as a dissertation for the degree of Doctor of Philosophy.

Joseph Duffy
Graduate Research Professor of
Mechanical Engineering

I certify that I have read this study and that in my opinion it conforms to acceptable standards of scholarly representation and is fully adequate, in scope and quality, as a dissertation for the degree of Doctor of Philosophy.

Jacob Hammer
Professor of Electrical Engineering

I certify that I have read this study and that in my opinion it conforms to acceptable standards of scholarly representation and is fully adequate, in scope and quality, as a dissertation for the degree of Doctor of Philosophy.

Boghos Sivazlian
Professor of Industrial and Systems
Engineering

I certify that I have read this study and that in my opinion it conforms to acceptable standards of scholarly representation and is fully adequate, in scope and quality, as a dissertation for the degree of Doctor of Philosophy.

Jack Smith
Professor of Electrical Engineering

This dissertation was submitted to the Graduate Faculty of the College of Engineering and to the Graduate School and was accepted as partial fulfillment of the requirements for the degree of Doctor of Philosophy.

December 1994

Winfred M. Phillips
Dean, College of Engineering

Karen A. Holbrook
Dean, Graduate School

Internet Distribution Consent Agreement

In reference to the following dissertation:

AUTHOR: Kalman, Andrew
TITLE: Software structures for digital remotely controlled systems (record number: 2042878)
PUBLICATION DATE: 1994

I, _____Andrew Kalman_____, as copyright holder for the aforementioned dissertation, hereby grant specific and limited archive and distribution rights to the Board of Trustees of the University of Florida and its agents. I authorize the University of Florida to digitize and distribute the dissertation described above for nonprofit, educational purposes via the Internet or successive technologies.

This is a non-exclusive grant of permissions for specific off-line and on-line uses for an indefinite term. Off-line uses shall be limited to those specifically allowed by "Fair Use" as prescribed by the terms of United States copyright legislation (cf, Title 17, U.S. Code) as well as to the maintenance and preservation of a digital archive copy. Digitization allows the University of Florida to generate image- and text-based versions as appropriate and to provide and enhance access using search software.

This grant of permissions prohibits use of the digitized versions for commercial use or profit

_____
Signature of Copyright Holder

_____Andrew Kalman_____
Printed or Typed Name of Copyright Holder/Licensee

personal information blurred

2008-06-19
Date of Signature

Please print, sign and return to:
Cathleen Martyniak
UF Dissertation Project
Preservation Department
University of Florida Libraries
P.O. Box 117007
Gainesville, FL 32611-7007

5/28/2008